Cordon Bleu

Vegetables

Cordon Bleu

Vegetables

CBC/B.P.C. Publishing Ltd.

Published by
B.P.C. Publishing Ltd.,
St. Giles House, 49 / 50 Poland Street,
London W1A 2LG

Designed by Melvyn Kyte
Printed by Proost, Turnhout, Belgium

These recipes have been adapted from the Cordon Bleu Cookery Course published by Purnell in association with the London Cordon Bleu Cookery School
Principal : Rosemary Hume ; Co-Principal : Muriel Downes

Contents

Introduction

Vegetables are the original 'instant food'. Picked young and fresh from the garden they need barely any cooking to make them edible, nourishing and delightful to the taste. Market produce will not be quite so young nor quite so fresh, and so will require slightly more preparation, but all in all the vegetable world provides us with a remarkable proportion of our daily food in a very readily accessible form.

We have included in this book many of the more unusual vegetables and have selected recipes that may be used either as an accompaniment to a main dish, as a first course, or in some cases as an entremets - adjust your quantities accordingly. You can do anything with vegetables, but remember the biggest sin of all is overcooking. Young, fresh vegetables, lightly cooked, contain a high proportion of vitamins and minerals that are essential to a healthy diet. Old, stale vegetables, or those that are cooked too long, not only lose these valuable nutrients but become dull and tasteless as well.

In the days before deep freezing the first spring vegetables were hailed as a welcome relief after the winter monotony of roots and the occasional cabbage. They are still unsurpassed, but frozen vegetables will help you ring the changes if you use them with discretion and are careful to cook them according to the directions on the packet.

Cordon Bleu cooks should shy away from the prize-winning giant vegetables shown with pride at horticultural shows — anything as big and old as these will never eat well, however attractive they look. But if you can persuade the kitchen gardening enthusiast in your family to let you gather the produce while it is young and tender, your meals will be the envy of your friends and the delight of your family.

Rosemary Hume
Muriel Downes

Globe artichokes

These are plentiful in the shops during the summer months but are good to grow yourself as they make decorative and handsome plants for the garden, look good in the herbaceous border and are delicious to eat when freshly picked. It is the buds of the artichoke that are eaten and there are one or two varieties specially suitable for the table. These have rounded tips to the leaves, rather than sharp prickles, which make for more comfortable handling.

Artichokes can be eaten hot with melted butter, or cold with a vinaigrette or French dressing, as a first course or as an entremets. They can also be stuffed and served as a more substantial first, or main, course.

To prepare : slice away any bottom stalk, then with the scissors snip off the points of the leaves. Wash thoroughly, then put into a large pan of boiling salted water. Boil gently for 25-45 minutes, according to the size of the artichoke. To test if the artichoke is cooked, pull out one of the leaves. If it comes away easily the artichoke is ready. Lift out with a draining spoon.

Serve them on individual hot plates. Globe artichokes are eaten with the fingers until the 'fond' is reached, then a small fork is used. Each leaf is pulled off and its fleshy end is dipped into melted butter or vinaigrette before being nibbled off ; the leaf is then discarded on your plate. Continue pulling off leaves and eating the ends until the 'choke' appears ; pull and scrape all of this gently away from the fond and discard it. Pour a little melted butter into the fond and season it before eating. Some people like 1-2 drops of lemon juice as well.

Really small artichokes, such as one finds abroad or can pick in the garden, are eaten whole, leaves and all, but they must, of course, be very young in order to do this. This is a rather extravagant way of using them unless you have several plants.

Tops of outer leaves of artichoke are snipped off before it is cooked

A leaf is peeled away to test if artichoke is cooked ; if it comes away easily, the artichoke is ready

Globe artichokes continued

Cooked artichoke ready to be served with French dressing

Artichokes alla barigoule

4 globe artichokes
$\frac{3}{4}$ lb flat mushrooms
$1\frac{1}{2}$ oz butter
1 medium-size carrot (finely chopped)
1 medium-size onion (finely chopped)
3 oz ham (chopped) — optional
2 tablespoons chopped parsley
1 tablespoon chopped mixed fresh herbs, or 1 dessertspoon of dried herbs (thyme, oregano, marjoram, etc.)
4-5 rounded tablespoons fresh white breadcrumbs
1 wineglass white wine
$\frac{1}{2}$ pint veal, or vegetable, stock
kneaded butter
salt and pepper

Barigoule is the name of a type of mushroom.

Method

Trim the artichokes, plunge into boiling salted water and cook for about 20-25 minutes, or until a leaf can be pulled out. Then drain and refresh ; leave to cool. Wash and chop the mushrooms, reserving 4 whole ones.

Melt the butter in a frying pan, put in the carrot and onion, cook slowly to soften a little, then add the chopped mushrooms. Continue to cook until most of the moisture has been driven off, approximately 5-6 minutes. Then draw aside, add the chopped ham (if using) and the parsley, herbs and enough of the crumbs to make a firm but moist mixture.

Set the oven at 350°F or Mark 4. Now pull out the centre leaves of the artichokes and carefully scrape out the chokes. Divide the mushroom mixture and fill the centres of the artichokes. Top each one with a whole mushroom and put a knob of butter on each. Arrange them in a deep ovenproof dish, pour around the white wine and stock. Cover with foil or buttered paper and cook in the pre-set oven for 35-40 minutes.

Take out of the oven and dish up the artichokes. Pour off the liquid — there should be about $7\frac{1}{2}$ fl oz. Thicken this liquid with a little kneaded butter to make a sauce the consistency of thin cream. Season sauce well and pour it round the artichokes.

Artichokes à la crème

1 can artichoke hearts
$\frac{3}{4}$ pint béchamel sauce
Parmesan cheese (grated) — for dusting

Buttered ramekins, or individual dishes

Method

Set oven at 400°F or Mark 6. Drain artichoke hearts, arrange in buttered dishes. Make béchamel sauce, pour over artichokes and dust with grated Parmesan. Bake in pre-set oven for 10-12 minutes, or until lightly browned.

Jerusalem artichokes belong to the sunflower family, the name being derived from *girasole*, the Italian for sunflower. They resemble nobbly potatoes and have an unusual and delicate flavour. They can be baked, steamed and served with béchamel sauce, cooked au gratin, or made into a soufflé.

Artichoke and tomato salad

1½ lb jerusalem artichokes
salted water
squeeze of lemon juice
4-5 tomatoes (according to size)

For dressing
1 carton (5 fl oz) plain yoghourt
2-3 tablespoons double cream
salt and pepper
1 teaspoon caster sugar
squeeze of lemon juice
1 dessertspoon snipped chives, or chopped parsley

Method

Peel artichokes and cut into walnut-size pieces. Cook in pan of salted water with a good squeeze of lemon juice until just tender (about 7-8 minutes). Drain, rinse in cold water and drain again. Put in a bowl with tomatoes (skinned, seeds removed, flesh shredded).

To prepare dressing : turn yoghourt into a bowl, whip the cream lightly, add to yoghourt with the seasoning, sugar and lemon juice. Add chives or parsley. Mix together with artichokes and tomatoes.

Arrange in a salad bowl or hors d'œuvre dish. Serve with brown bread and butter.

Artichokes au gratin duxelles

2 lb jerusalem artichokes
milk and water (in equal proportions, enough to cover artichokes)
6 oz flat mushrooms
1 onion
1 oz butter
1 oz plain flour
salt and pepper
2-3 tablespoons creamy milk
1 tablespoon browned breadcrumbs
1-2 tablespoons grated cheese

Method

Peel artichokes and put them in a pan. Cover with milk and water mixture, simmer for 7-10 minutes, or until just tender, drain and put into a fireproof gratin dish. Retain ½ pint of the artichoke liquid for the sauce. Set oven at 375-400°F or Mark 5-6.

Wash and chop mushrooms finely. Do not peel or remove the stalks. Chop the onion, melt butter in a pan, add onion and mushrooms, cover and cook slowly for 3-4 minutes. Then take off lid and boil hard to remove some of the moisture.

Draw aside, stir in the flour and pour on the artichoke liquid. Stir over heat until boiling and cook for 2 minutes. Season and finish with creamy milk. Spoon this sauce over the artichokes and scatter over some browned crumbs and then the grated cheese.

Cook in a pre-set oven for about 10 minutes, or until evenly browned.

Note : if you prefer to use fewer artichokes, place a layer of sliced, hard-boiled egg at the bottom of the dish.

Asparagus

Asparagus is a favourite in this country as a luxury vegetable. It is on the whole fairly expensive to buy.

English asparagus comes into season in the middle of May and lasts to the end of June. It has a dark green stem and head with a small proportion of white and a thinner stem than the continental kind. French and Belgian asparagus is earlier. There are many varieties, the most famous one being the French Argenteuil ; this can be recognised by the thick stems with a green or pinky brown head and white stalk. Sprue is a thinner variety of asparagus.

Asparagus is served as a first course or an entremets (after the main course) with melted butter or a hollandaise sauce, or maltaise sauce which is flavoured with orange.

Asparagus is sold in bundles and in some shops loose by the pound, which is cheaper. To prepare, cut away about 2 inches or so of the bottom stalks, leaving about 2-3 inches before the green starts. Cut while still tied in bundles (or gather the loose asparagus together) to ensure that all stalks are of the same length. Then, with a small vegetable knife, scrape the white part of the stems well, and put into a bowl of cold water. When all are done, gather the asparagus together, about 8-12 at a time, according to size, and tie in bundles with fine string.

Leave the cut stems in water until ready to cook. Then cook gently in plenty of boiling salted water, stalk end down but with the tips barely immersed and the lid off the pan, for 12-15 minutes or until the green part is tender. If the tips are out of the water, cook them with the lid of the pan on. Lift out carefully, drain well on a piece of muslin, then place on a folded napkin, cutting the string of each bundle just before serving. Accompany with an appropriate sauce.

Asparagus with anchovy sauce

1-2 bundles of asparagus
2 oz butter
1 oz onion (chopped)
1 oz shallot (chopped)
1 oz mushroom peelings and stalks
1 dessertspoon mixed chopped herbs (parsley, thyme, tarragon)
1 glass white wine
$\frac{1}{2}$ pint fish stock
1 glass Madeira, or sherry
2 egg yolks
anchovy essence
salt and pepper

Method

Cook asparagus as instructed on page 13. Melt $\frac{1}{2}$ oz butter in a pan, add onion, shallot, mushrooms and herbs. Cover and simmer for 5-7 minutes. Add the white wine and fish stock and simmer for a further 10-15 minutes, skimming occasionally.

Strain sauce and return to the rinsed out pan. Boil rapidly to reduce by about one third. Add the Madeira, or sherry, and set over a pan of hot water. Beat the egg yolks with a nut of butter, add a spoonful of the hot sauce and pour it back slowly into the pan. Add the rest of the butter slowly in small pieces.

Add a few drops of anchovy essence and season carefully to taste. Serve separately in a sauce boat.

Asparagus with hollandaise sauce

1-2 bundles of asparagus

For hollandaise sauce
4 tablespoons wine vinegar
6 peppercorns
1 blade of mace
1 slice of onion
$\frac{1}{2}$ bayleaf
3 egg yolks
5 oz butter
pinch of salt
1-2 tablespoons cream, or top of milk
squeeze of lemon juice (optional)

Method

Cook asparagus as instructed on page 13.

Put the wine vinegar into a small pan with peppercorns, mace, onion and bayleaf. Boil this liquid until it is reduced to a scant tablespoon, then set pan aside.

Cream egg yolks in a bowl with a good $\frac{1}{2}$ oz butter and a pinch of salt. Strain the vinegar mixture on to this and set the bowl over a pan of boiling water. Turn off the heat under the pan, then add remaining butter in small pieces to the egg mixture, stirring vigorously all the time.

Watchpoint When you add the butter, it should be slightly soft, not straight from the refrigerator.

When all the butter has been added and the sauce is thick, taste for seasoning and add 1-2 tablespoons of cream (or top of the milk) and a squeeze of lemon juice (optional). Pleasantly sharp yet bland, the sauce should have the consistency of thick cream.

Drain asparagus and place on a folded napkin. Serve sauce separately in a sauce boat.

Argenteuil tartlets

4 oz quantity of shortcrust pastry

For filling
1 bundle of asparagus (about 16 spears)
1 packet of Demi-Sel cheese
salt and pepper
2 tablespoons French dressing
1 teaspoon mixed chopped herbs

16 small boat moulds

Method
Roll out the shortcrust pastry, line the greased boat moulds with it and bake blind. Leave them to cool, then turn out of the moulds.

Cook the asparagus, refresh and leave to drain on a piece of muslin.

Season the cream cheese and fill into the pastry cases, levelling it with a palette knife. Trim each asparagus spear to the size of the boat moulds and spoon over the French dressing and herbs. Arrange a spear of asparagus on top of the cheese in each pastry case.

Asparagus rolls

Cut crust off a small brown loaf ; butter and cut into thin slices. Place a cooked asparagus head on each slice and roll up.

Asparagus nordaise

1 bundle of asparagus
2 oz mushrooms
$1\frac{1}{4}$ oz butter
salt and pepper
$\frac{1}{2}$ oz plain flour
5 fl oz top of milk
$1\frac{1}{2}$ oz cheese (grated)
hot buttered toast (for serving)

This quantity makes approximately 8 servings.

Method
Trim, cook and drain the asparagus. Wash and cut the mushrooms into thick slices, add to $\frac{3}{4}$ oz of the butter, melted, season and cook slowly with the pan lid on for 5-6 minutes.

Melt the remaining $\frac{1}{2}$ oz butter in a pan, add the flour off the heat and then pour on the milk. Stir sauce until boiling ; add the cheese and seasoning.

Arrange the mushrooms, and then 1-2 asparagus tips, on fingers of hot buttered toast. Spoon sauce over each one and glaze them under the grill.

Aubergines

Aubergines, also known as egg plants, are distinguished by their purple skins (though other varieties do exist). They are used unpeeled and are salted and drained before cooking, to remove excess moisture and any bitterness. Sliced and fried, they make an excellent accompaniment to grills and fried chicken.

They can also be served as a separate course, stuffed, or mixed with other vegetables as a salad — for instance salad niçoise, or ratatouille.

They are available at most times of the year, imported from different countries.

Aubergines Boston

2 even-size aubergines
olive oil
1 medium-size onion
1 oz butter
salt and pepper
5 oz cooked ham (thinly sliced and shredded)
½ pint béchamel sauce
1 tablespoon cream (optional)
1 oz cheese (grated)

Method

Split aubergines in two lengthways, run the point of a knife round the inside of the skin and score across the flesh. Sprinkle with salt and leave for 30 minutes. Set oven at 375°F or Mark 5.

Dry the aubergines and fry in hot oil on the cut surface until brown. Put in the pre-set oven for 5-10 minutes to soften completely.

Meanwhile chop the onion and soften it in the butter in a covered pan. Scoop out the aubergine flesh carefully, chop it a little and add to the onion. Season, cook for a few minutes until soft, then add the ham. Put back into the skins and set on a baking tray. Prepare béchamel, adding cream if wished, and coat aubergines. Sprinkle with cheese and brown in hot oven at 425°F or Mark 7 for 8-10 minutes.

Aubergines

Brinjals

- 2 large aubergines
- 1 tablespoon oil
- 2 onions
- 3 green chillies, or 1 green pepper (chopped)
- ½ teaspoon cumin seeds
- salt
- caster sugar (to taste)
- juice of 1 lemon
- 1 lime, or 1 lemon (sliced)

Method

Set oven at 350°F or Mark 4. Rub the aubergines with oil, wrap in greaseproof paper and bake in pre-set oven for 30-40 minutes, or until soft. Scrape out the pulp of the aubergines and mash well. Mince or grate one of the onions and add to the aubergines with the chillies (or pepper). Season, add sugar to taste and sharpen with lemon juice. Chill the mixture, and turn into a serving dish; decorate with the second onion, cut into very thin rings, and slices of lime or lemon. Serve as an accompaniment to curry.

Note: cooked marrow pulp or a mashed cooked cucumber may be prepared in the same way.

Aubergines alla napolitana

6 medium-size aubergines
olive oil
4 tomatoes
2 red peppers
2 oz butter
6 rounded tablespoons fresh white breadcrumbs
1 tablespoon chopped parsley
4 anchovy fillets
2 tablespoons capers
2 oz black olives (stoned and chopped)
salt and pepper
1 dessertspoon fresh, or 1 teaspoon dried, oregano
$\frac{1}{2}$ lb Mozzarella, or Bel Paese, cheese (sliced)

Mozzarella cheese is difficult to obtain in this country, but Bel Paese makes an excellent substitute.

Method

Wash and dry the aubergines and cut lengthwise, salt the cut surface lightly and leave for 30 minutes. Dry with absorbent paper and fry lightly in oil to brown the cut surface. Scrape out the insides of the aubergines, leaving just the skin. Scald and skin the tomatoes, remove the seeds and cut the flesh into strips. Skin the peppers and take out the seeds ; cut flesh into strips and blanch these. Melt the butter in a pan and gently fry the breadcrumbs, chopped parsley, anchovies, capers and chopped olives. Season and add the oregano and 2 tablespoons of olive oil.

Set the oven at 350°F or Mark 4. Mix the stuffing mixture with the insides of the aubergines and fill back into the aubergine skins, smoothing over with a knife. Place some strips of pepper and tomato on each stuffed half. Put some oil into a roasting tin and add the aubergines. Baste each one with oil and cook in the pre-set oven for 1 hour. Five minutes before serving, take out and put a slice of Mozzarella cheese and a nut of butter on top of each stuffed half. Return to a hot oven, or place under the grill, for 3-5 minutes until cheese is just melted.

Stuffed aubergines (Aubergines farcies)

2 aubergines
4 lambs kidneys
$1\frac{1}{2}$ oz butter
2 medium-size onions (finely sliced)
1 dessertspoon plain flour
1 teaspoon tomato purée
$\frac{1}{4}$ pint stock
1 clove of garlic (crushed with $\frac{1}{2}$ teaspoon salt)
salt and pepper
1 bayleaf
$\frac{1}{2}$ lb tomatoes
2-3 tablespoons salad oil
1 tablespoon grated cheese (preferably Parmesan)
1 tablespoon fresh white breadcrumbs

Method

Split aubergines in two lengthways, score round edge and across, salt and leave for 30 minutes to dégorger.

Skin the kidneys and cut out cores, cut in half lengthways. Heat a small sauté pan, drop in half the butter and, when foaming, put in the kidneys. Brown quickly on all sides then remove from the pan and keep warm. Lower the heat, add remaining butter and the onion. Cook for 2-3 minutes then draw aside. Stir in the flour, tomato purée and stock and bring to the boil. Add the crushed garlic to the pan with pepper, bayleaf and the kidneys. Cover and simmer gently for about 20 minutes.

Wipe the aubergines dry and sauté rather slowly in 2-3 tablespoons of oil until soft.

Watchpoint Aubergines brown very quickly when sautéd. If the flesh is browned before being cooked right through, complete cooking in oven.

Skin the tomatoes, remove the seeds and roughly chop flesh. When the aubergines are tender, scoop out the pulp with a spoon, leaving the skins intact.

Remove bayleaf from the kidneys, add the tomatoes and aubergine pulp and simmer together for 2-3 minutes. Set the aubergine skins in an ovenproof dish, fill with the mixture and dust the tops with the cheese and crumbs. Brown in oven, pre-set at 425°F or Mark 7, for approximately 7 minutes.

Aubergine with crab

2 good-size aubergines
6-7 oz crab claw meat
salt and pepper
oil
2 medium-size onions
1 dessertspoon paprika pepper
1 tablespoon tomato purée
½ lb ripe tomatoes (skinned, seeds removed, and sliced)
½ teaspoon oregano
pinch of cayenne pepper, or drop of Tabasco sauce
2 tablespoons grated Parmesan and Gruyère cheese (mixed)
1-2 tablespoons melted butter

Method

Split aubergines in two lengthways, score, sprinkle with salt and leave for 30 minutes. Set oven at 350°F or Mark 4.

Wipe aubergines dry, then brown the cut surface in a little hot oil; take out, set on a baking tin and cook in pre-set oven until tender (about 10 minutes).

Meanwhile slice onions and soften in 2-3 tablespoons oil; add paprika and after a few seconds add tomato purée, tomatoes, oregano and cayenne (or Tabasco). Season and cook to a rich pulp. Scoop out the pulp from the cooked aubergines, add it to the pan and continue to cook for a few minutes. Then flake the crab meat with a fork and add it to the pan. Pile this mixture into the aubergine skins, sprinkle well with cheese and melted butter and brown in oven, at 425°F or Mark 7, for 6-7 minutes.

Casserole of aubergine

2 aubergines (sliced)
salt
oil (for frying)
1 small can ($2\frac{1}{2}$-3 fl oz) vegetable, or tomato, sauce
1 carton (5 fl oz) plain yoghourt
black pepper (ground from mill)

Serve with grills or sauté slices of liver.

Method

Score the sliced aubergines lightly with a knife, sprinkle with salt and leave for 30 minutes. Set the oven at 350°F or Mark 4.

Dry the aubergine slices, heat the oil and fry aubergine until golden brown on each side. Put the slices as they come from the pan into a casserole, layering them with the vegetable sauce and yoghourt, season with black pepper. Cover and bake in the pre-set oven for about 40 minutes. Turn out for serving.

Galette of aubergines

4-5 aubergines
about 8 tablespoons olive oil
1 clove of garlic (crushed)
1 medium-size onion (finely chopped)
1 lb ripe tomatoes, or 1 can (about 14 oz) Italian tomatoes
1 tablespoon tomato purée
salt and pepper
1 carton (5 fl oz) plain yoghourt
$\frac{1}{2}$ wineglass stock

7-inch diameter cake tin

Make this dish when tomatoes and aubergines are plentiful and inexpensive.

Method

Wipe the aubergines and cut in diagonal slices, sprinkle with salt and leave for 30 minutes. Heat 2 tablespoons of oil in a saucepan, add garlic and onion and fry slowly for 3-4 minutes. Then add tomatoes, skinned, seeds removed, and chopped (or the contents of the can) and the purée. Season and cook to a thick pulp. Set aside.

Set oven at 350°F or Mark 4.

Wipe aubergine slices, then fry until brown in the remaining

Spreading yoghourt over layer of tomato pulp and aubergine slices for galette of aubergines

oil. Have ready the cake tin, arrange a layer of aubergines on the bottom, spread with a little tomato pulp and a little yoghourt. Continue in this way until all the aubergines slices are in. Do not flavour the top layer of aubergines. Reserve about a third of the tomato pulp and add the stock to this ; set aside.

Cover the aubergines with a piece of foil or greaseproof paper, press down lightly, then bake in the pre-set oven for 40-45 minutes. Leave tin for a few minutes before turning out galette. Boil up sauce, pour it over the galette and serve.

Turning out the cooked galette of aubergines on to a serving dish

Lamb chops with aubergine

2 lamb chops, or 1 large gigot chop
2 tablespoons oil
1 oz butter
2 onions (sliced)
1 medium-size aubergine (sliced and lightly salted)
salt and pepper
1 clove of garlic (crushed)
1 teaspoon tomato purée
1 wineglass stock
3-4 tomatoes (skinned, sliced and seeds removed)
2 tablespoons grated cheese
1 tablespoon chopped parsley

Method

Set the oven at 350°F or Mark 4. Heat the oil and butter and fry the lamb chops quickly on both sides to brown them well. Then remove chops from pan.

Reheat frying pan, add a little more oil if necessary and fry the onions until turning brown. Take them out and put in the drained aubergine slices and fry for 5-6 minutes, turning frequently. Replace the onions and season ; add garlic, tomato purée, stock and tomatoes. Bring to the boil. Turn half of this mixture into an ovenproof casserole (or flameproof one if using the top of the stove), place chops on top and cover with rest of the aubergine and tomato mixture. Dust the top with grated cheese, and put dish uncovered into the pre-set oven (or cook covered on top of the stove) for about 35-40 minutes. Dust the top thickly with parsley and serve hot with potatoes.

Aubergine cream

4 medium-size aubergines (about $1\frac{1}{2}$ lb)
6 oz cooked ham (half fat, half lean)
chopped parsley
4 eggs (separated)
scant 2 oz Gruyère cheese (grated)
salt and pepper

For béchamel sauce
1 oz butter
$\frac{3}{4}$ oz plain flour
good $\frac{1}{4}$ pint flavoured milk
salt and pepper

tomato sauce (for serving)

Charlotte tin, or ring mould ($1\frac{1}{2}$ pints capacity)

Method

Peel aubergines, dice them and boil in pan of salted water for 4-5 minutes. When barely tender, drain aubergines thoroughly, then mash. Chop ham also and add to the aubergines with the parsley. Set oven at 400°F or Mark 6.

Make the béchamel sauce, stir in the egg yolks, and add the aubergine mixture, cheese and seasoning. Whip egg whites firmly and fold into the mixture. Turn it into the well greased tin (or mould) and cook in pre-set oven for about 25-30 minutes until well browned. Serve in the tin (or mould) or turn out, and pour round a tomato sauce.

Haricots verts béarnais

1 lb packet of sliced, or whole, frozen haricot beans
4 rashers of back bacon
$\frac{1}{2}$ oz butter
1 medium-size onion (finely chopped)
black pepper (ground from mill)

Method

Cook the beans following the instructions on the packet; drain and refresh them with cold water. Drain well. Remove the rind and rust from the bacon and cut into $\frac{1}{2}$-inch strips, set aside. Melt the butter in a sauté pan, add the onion and cook slowly until soft but not coloured, then add the bacon to the pan, increase the heat and fry until the bacon is crisp and the onion brown. Tip the beans into the pan and toss until hot, adding black pepper from the mill.

Broad beans Marie Anne

2 lb young broad beans (podded)
1 bunch of baby carrots
$\frac{1}{2}$ oz butter

For poulette sauce
1 oz butter
1 tablespoon plain flour
$\frac{1}{4}$ pint strong chicken stock
salt and pepper
1 egg yolk
2-3 tablespoons double cream
1 teaspoon chopped savory
1 teaspoon chopped parsley

This dish makes a good first course.

Method

Shell the beans, leave the carrots whole with a small portion of the green part on or, if they are large, quarter them. Cook beans and carrots separately in small quantities of water for 15-20 minutes, then drain, mix them together in the butter and draw pan aside.

To prepare poulette sauce: melt the butter in a pan, stir in the flour and cook for five seconds; then draw pan aside, cool slightly, pour in the stock, blend, stir until sauce is boiling, cook for 2-3 minutes and season. Blend egg yolk and cream and add gradually to the sauce with the herbs.

Heat sauce carefully, without boiling, and pour it on to the beans and carrots; return pan to heat and shake gently until vegetables are very hot but do not allow sauce to boil again. Turn vegetables into a dish for serving.

Flageolets toulousaine

1 can (about 15 oz) flageolets
1 tablespoon oil, or 1 oz butter
2 or more cloves of garlic (crushed with salt)
3 ripe tomatoes (scalded, skinned, seeds removed)
salt and pepper

In this country it is easier to buy canned than fresh flageolets. They are delicious, small green kidney beans, much used in France.

Method

Put the oil (or butter) into a pan or flameproof serving dish, add the garlic and tomatoes and soften to a pulp. Then add the flageolets (drained) and season. Cover and simmer for 7-10 minutes, or until all the ingredients are thoroughly mixed. Serve hot.

Pea beans

The pods of the bean have more pronounced beans in them than the French or runner beans.

Gather the pods when the beans in them can be felt but before they become too large. To cook : top and tail them and cook whole or cut in half like French beans, then cook in the same way. Finish with butter and serve as an accompanying vegetable. If wished, the pods may be allowed to mature, the beans taken out, dried and stored as haricots.

Waxpod beans

Many visitors to the Continent have learnt to appreciate the fine qualities of the waxpod bean (sometimes known as butter beans). The yellow pods are usually cooked whole, in the same way as French beans. These butter beans should not be confused with the seeds purchased from grocery stores under the name of butter beans (which are imported) as they will not mature in the unfavourable climate of the British Isles.

Cook as for French beans.

Mung beans

These beans produce sprouts (or shoots) which can be bought in some supermarkets, but which can easily and more cheaply be grown at home. The beans themselves can be bought from most seedsmen. The sprouts are used in Chinese recipes, or they can accompany a grill or roast.

To cook : pick over and wash them thoroughly, then put into plenty of boiling salted water. Boil 3-4 minutes until barely tender (they should remain lightly crisp). Then drain well and return to pan with $\frac{1}{2}$ oz butter, salt and pepper. Shake over heat then serve.

Alternatively wash and dry sprouts ; sauté them over brisk heat in 2-3 tablespoons hot oil for about 5 minutes, shaking and turning frequently.

Preparation of dried beans

1 Wash the vegetables and pick them over to remove any grit or small stones.
2 Soak them in plenty of tepid water for 8 hours, or leave overnight. If they have to be left longer, change the water or they may start to ferment.
3 Allow 2-3 oz vegetables per person (weight before soaking).
4 Drain them, cover with plenty of fresh warm water and cook in a covered pan. If the water is hard, add a pinch of bicarbonate of soda which will help to soften the outer skins. Salt is never added at this stage as it would harden them. Bring them very slowly to boiling point, allowing 30-40 minutes, then simmer gently for about 1 hour. Drain them again and then use as specified in the recipe.

Chilli con carne

6 oz red beans (soaked and pre-cooked, see page 27)
1 lb minced steak
2 tablespoons oil, or dripping
2 onions (finely chopped)
2 tablespoons chilli con carne spice, or 1 dessertspoon chilli powder
1 dessertspoon paprika pepper

Method

Choose a large stew pan or deep frying pan, heat the dripping in this, add onion and when it is about to turn colour, add the spices. Add the mince, stirring for 4-5 minutes, then add the drained beans and a little of their cooking liquor.

Cover and simmer until beef and beans are tender (about $1\frac{1}{2}$ hours). During this time the pan should be covered and if the mixture gets too thick add a little of the water. The consistency should be that of a rich stew.

Boston baked beans

1 lb dried pea beans
2 pints water
2 teaspoons dry mustard
$\frac{1}{4}$ teaspoon black, or white, pepper
1 tablespoon salt
3 medium-size onions
1 tablespoon black treacle
1 tablespoon golden syrup
2 oz soft brown sugar
$\frac{1}{2}$ lb salt belly pork

Method

Pick over and wash the beans in several changes of water, then soak overnight in 1 pint of the measured water.

Set oven at 250°F or Mark $\frac{1}{2}$. Mix the mustard, pepper and salt with 1 pint water in a large casserole and tip in the beans with their soaking liquor. Quarter the onions and add to the casserole with the treacle, syrup and brown sugar. Cover and put in pre-set oven to bake for 6-8 hours.

Soak the pork in cold water for 1 hour, then blanch for 10 minutes. Remove the skin, cut into small strips, add to casserole and continue cooking for about 1 hour or until the meat is very tender.

If necessary, add extra water at the same time as the pork. Remove the lid of casserole for last 30 minutes.

Adding quartered onions to the casserole containing soaked beans

Removing the skin from salt belly pork before adding to the beans

Boston baked beans after they have been cooked with salt belly pork

Cassoulet

1 lb dried haricot beans (soaked and pre-cooked, see page 27)
6 oz salt belly pork, or green streaky bacon
4 cloves of garlic (finely chopped)
$\frac{1}{2}$ shoulder of mutton, or half a duck
2 tablespoons good beef dripping, or bacon fat, or butter
bouquet garni
salt and black pepper
4 oz garlic, or pork, sausage
$\frac{3}{4}$ lb ripe tomatoes, or 1 medium-size can
1 dessertspoon tomato purée
1 teaspoon sugar
browned breadcrumbs

This is a traditional dish from the Languedoc region of France and it contains many specialities of that region. The recipe here is simplified with mutton to replace the traditional pickled goose. If preferred, half a duck could be used. Garlic sausage can be obtained at most delicatessens, or you can use a pork sausage.

Method

Drain the beans and put into a large flameproof casserole with the pork or bacon and the finely chopped garlic. Pour in water to cover well, put on lid, simmer gently for 1-$1\frac{1}{4}$ hours. Drain, set aside and reserve liquor.

Bone the mutton and cut into large cubes or leave the duck in one piece. Fry until golden-brown in the dripping, add the beans and pork to the casserole with the herbs and a little salt, and a lot of black pepper. Moisten with some of the bean liquor, cover and stew very slowly for 3-4 hours, adding a little more of the cooking liquor from time to time, if necessary. After $2\frac{1}{2}$ hours cooking, add the sausage. When the beans are tender, take out pork, remove skin and slice; also slice the sausage; replace pork (or bacon) and sausage in casserole.

Cook the tomatoes to a pulp in a separate pan, add the tomato purée and season with salt, pepper and sugar. Spoon this mixture over the beans, shake the casserole gently to mix it in, then sprinkle the top of the beans with the browned crumbs. Put in oven, pre-set at 375°F or Mark 5, for a further $\frac{3}{4}$-1 hour to brown.

Puchero bean stew (with pork and tomatoes)

½ lb red, or brown, beans (soaked overnight in plenty of water)
1 lb salt belly of pork (or beef flank, or brisket)
2 tablespoons salad oil
1 large onion (peeled and sliced)
1 large carrot (peeled and sliced)
1-2 cloves of garlic (chopped)
1 dessertspoon tomato purée
1-1½ pints stock, or water
pepper
bouquet garni
2 caps of pimiento (sliced)
½ lb ripe tomatoes (peeled and halved)
2 saveloys, or equivalent in smoked sausage (about 6 oz)

Puchero (a stew) is a dish of Spanish origin, and there are several versions but this particular recipe comes from South America.

Method

Drain beans, put into a large pan, well cover with cold water and bring slowly to the boil. Simmer for 1½ hours.

Meanwhile put the meat in a separate pan of cold water, bring to the boil and continue cooking for about 1 hour. Then drain both the beans and meat.

Heat oil in the pan in which the beans were cooked, add onion and carrot slices and garlic. Cook for 4-5 minutes, then add beans, tomato purée and stock (or water). Add a little pepper but no salt. Bring pan to the boil, put in meat, add bouquet garni, cover and simmer until beans and meat are tender (about 1½ hours). After 1 hour add the prepared pimiento and tomatoes.

Blanch sausages by putting in cold water, bringing to boil and draining. Then add to the stew and continue to simmer. The puchero should be thick and rich by this time; if too thick, add a little extra stock.

Before dishing up, take out meat and sausages and slice them. Return slices to the puchero. Adjust seasoning and turn the stew into a deep serving dish or casserole.

Haricot beans with sausages

$\frac{1}{2}$ lb dried haricot beans (soaked and pre-cooked, see page 27)
1 lb pork sausages
$1\frac{1}{2}$ oz butter
1 medium-size onion (finely chopped)
1 dessertspoon plain flour
2 tablespoons stock
1 wineglass white wine
salt and pepper
squeeze of lemon juice

Method

Fry the sausages until cooked and brown on all sides, then add the beans and cook until they are slightly browned and have absorbed the fat from the sausages; turn them into a casserole.

Melt 1 oz butter in a pan, add the onion and cook until brown; stir in the flour, stock and wine, season and bring to the boil. Cook for 10 minutes, add a squeeze of lemon juice and pour sauce over the beans and sausages. Dot the remaining $\frac{1}{2}$ oz of butter over the beans and shake well until absorbed. Serve very hot and well seasoned.

Butter beans maître d'hôtel

$\frac{1}{2}$ lb butter beans (soaked and pre-cooked, see page 27)
$\frac{1}{4}$ lb salt belly pork
1 onion (stuck with a clove)
bouquet garni
$1\frac{1}{2}$ oz butter
1 clove of garlic (crushed)
1 tablespoon chopped parsley
juice of $\frac{1}{2}$ lemon
black pepper (ground from mill)

Method

Put beans in a pan with fresh water to cover, add the pork, onion and bouquet garni; simmer for 1 hour.

Strain off the liquid, reserving $\frac{1}{4}$ pint of the cooking liquor, discard the onion and bouquet garni. Remove the rind from the pork, then cut the flesh into strips. Return the beans and pork to the pan, add the reserved cooking liquor and heat it gently.

Cream the butter with the crushed garlic, parsley, lemon juice and black pepper, and drop it into the pan in pieces. Turn off the heat under the pan and shake it gently until the butter has melted and mixed with the beans, then serve.

Butter beans ménagère

½ lb butter beans (soaked and pre-cooked, see page 27)
2 sticks of celery (sliced)
1 onion (sliced)
1 bayleaf
salt and pepper
1 tablespoon chopped parsley
2 tablespoons double cream
1 large tomato (skinned and sliced)
1 tablespoon caster sugar
¼ oz butter

For white sauce
1½ oz butter
1 oz plain flour
½ pint milk

Method

Put prepared beans in a pan with celery, onion and bayleaf ; cover with boiling water, season and cook for 30-40 minutes until tender.

Meanwhile prepare a white sauce with the butter, flour, milk and seasoning.

Drain the vegetables, remove the bayleaf and reserve about ¼ pint of the cooking liquor. Add the vegetables to the white sauce, shake the pan gently to mix, add the parsley and cream and the reserved cooking liquor. Taste for seasoning and tip the mixture into a hot gratin dish.

Dust the tomato slices with salt, pepper and caster sugar, dot with ¼ oz butter and grill. Arrange them on top of the beans and serve.

Butter beans served in a creamy tomato sauce with a tomato garnish

Haricot beans with cream sauce

4 oz dried haricot beans
1 teaspoon bicarbonate of soda to 2 quarts boiling water (for soaking)
1 head of celery (sliced)
8 oz button onions
1 tablespoon chopped parsley

For $\frac{3}{4}$ pint cream sauce
$1\frac{1}{2}$ oz butter
$1\frac{1}{2}$ oz plain flour
$\frac{3}{4}$ pint milk
salt and pepper
2-3 tablespoons single cream

Method

Wash the beans in several changes of water. Pour on the boiling water (with bicarbonate of soda) and leave beans to soak overnight.

After soaking, rinse the beans well and place in a pan with celery and whole onions. Cover with cold water and bring very slowly to the boil. Simmer gently for about 1 hour until beans are tender.

To prepare the sauce : melt butter, stir in flour off the heat and add milk ; blend, season well and add the cream. Return to heat and boil.

Drain the vegetables and add to the sauce with the chopped parsley. Turn into a casserole for serving.

Boiling and baking

To boil beetroot : scrub well but be careful not to break skin or it will 'bleed' and lose colour. Boil for about $1\frac{1}{2}$ hours. To test if done, take out and rub off a small piece of skin. If it comes away easily beetroot is cooked. Cool in liquid then peel.

To bake beetroot : wrap it in foil or greaseproof paper and bake in oven at 350°F or Mark 4, for 2-3 hours. This takes longer than boiling but gives a good flavour. Test as for boiling, and leave to cool before peeling.

Creamed beetroot

1 bunch of baby beetroots (a bunch usually holds 6-8)
½ oz butter
1 tablespoon freshly grated horseradish
salt and pepper
1-2 tablespoons double cream

For white sauce
1½ oz butter
scant 1½ oz plain flour
1 pint milk

Method

Prepare beetroots by trimming off the stalks, but do not cut the root itself in any way. Plunge beetroots into a pan of boiling, salted water and boil for 35-40 minutes or until the skins can be rubbed off with your thumb. Then drain them, rub off skins and replace beetroots in pan with the butter.

Prepare the white sauce and simmer it until it has the consistency of cream. Add the horseradish, seasoning and the cream.

Reheat beetroots, turn into a vegetable dish and spoon on the sauce ; serve very hot.

Beetroot relish

2 large cooked beetroots
2 tart dessert, or cooking, apples
3-4 tablespoons French dressing (with a little garlic added)

Method

Grate the beetroot coarsely ; peel, quarter and core the apples and cut into dice. Mix with the beetroot and moisten with a little of the French dressing. Pile into a dish for serving.

Beetroot and horseradish relish

6-8 large cooked beetroots (about 2 lb)
4 oz finely grated horseradish (fresh, or bottled variety preserved in vinegar only and drained)
1 teaspoon dry mustard
½ teaspoon salt
½ teaspoon black pepper
1 tablespoon caster sugar
3 tablespoons red wine vinegar
½ pint soured cream, or ½ pint double cream (soured with about ½ teaspoon lemon juice)

Method

Grate the beetroot and mix with the horseradish. Mix all the seasonings and sugar with the wine vinegar and stir into the soured cream. Mix in the beetroot and horseradish and turn into bowls for serving.

Broccoli

Purple-sprouting broccoli is easily obtainable in the shops in September and early October. This broccoli has a handsome purple head the size of a small cauliflower. The flavour is excellent and, served with a hollandaise sauce, broccoli makes a good first course or entremets.
Italian broccoli (calabrese). This is similar to the purple-sprouting broccoli but is in season earlier, towards the end of July and during August. The central small head is green, with a very delicate flavour.

The side shoots may be trimmed of leaves, tied in bundles and cooked like asparagus. Serve calabrese with melted or noisette butter; alternatively the smaller shoots may be well blanched, then drained, dipped into fritter batter and fried. Serve plain or with a hollandaise sauce.

Both types of broccoli are recommended for deep freezing.

Italian broccoli au gratin

3-4 hearts of Italian broccoli (according to size)
grated cheese

For sauce
1 oz butter
1 oz plain flour
1 shallot (finely chopped)
$\frac{1}{2}$ pint chicken stock (free of fat)
1 egg yolk (for liaison)
2-3 tablespoons double cream (for liaison)
1 dessertspoon French mustard (preferably Grey Poupon)
squeeze of lemon juice

Italian broccoli or calabrese is well suited to a first course for a summer lunch.

Method

Wash broccoli thoroughly, then cook in boiling salted water for about 20 minutes until it is barely tender. Drain it well. Lay it in a well-buttered gratin dish and keep warm while preparing the sauce.

Melt butter, cook shallot until soft, stir in flour and cook for about 5 seconds. Draw pan aside and cook slightly before pouring on stock. Blend, return to heat and bring to boil. Cook for 4-5 minutes until it just coats the spoon. Mix egg yolk and cream and stir into the sauce; add lemon juice and mustard.

Draw pan aside, cool sauce for 1 minute, then beat in the cheese, reserving about 1 tablespoon. Coat broccoli with the sauce, sprinkle with remaining cheese and brown under the grill. Serve hot.

Red brussels sprouts

If there is room in the garden, grow a row of these sprouts. They are small, tight and compact and dark red in colour, turning to a deep green when cooked. Cook them in the usual way (see right) but do not make a cross cut on the bottom. They should be just done — *not* over-cooked. Serve as an accompanying vegetable.

Brussels sprouts with celery

1-1½ lb sprouts
1 stick of celery
1½ oz butter
1 onion (chopped)
1 oz plain flour
¾ pint milk
a little extra butter, melted
2 tablespoons dried breadcrumbs

Method

Prepare and boil the sprouts (see right). Blanch the celery in boiling water for 1 minute and chop. Melt the butter, add onion and celery and cook gently for a few minutes, to soften.

Stir in the flour and then blend in the milk. Add the cooked sprouts and continue cooking for a few minutes then turn into an ovenproof dish. Sprinkle with melted butter and breadcrumbs and brown in a hot oven, pre-set at 400°F or Mark 6, for 10 minutes.

Brussels sprouts

1½ lb small sprouts, or 2 lb large sprouts
salt
½-1 oz butter
black pepper (ground from mill)

Method

Trim the sprouts, removing any loose outside leaves and wash well in cold salted water. Drain. Cook uncovered in a large pan of boiling salted water until just tender, no longer than 8 minutes after the water has reboiled. Drain well and return to the pan with a knob of butter and cook for 2-3 minutes. If you cook them this way, do not use more than ½-1 oz butter.

Watchpoint Never keep sprouts hot for a long time and, if entertaining, cook early in the day without butter and, after draining, refresh thoroughly with cold water. This will set the bright green colour of the sprouts and prevent any unpleasant smell, which is only caused by overcooking and keeping them warm. Just before dishing up, put the sprouts in a large pan — they will heat more quickly if only in a single layer, and set on a steady heat. When the steam stops rising, drop in ½-1 oz butter in small pieces and shake the pan over the heat until the butter melts, rolling the sprouts round to coat them with the butter. Season with black pepper and dish up at once.

Brussels sprouts with chestnuts

$1\frac{1}{2}$ lb brussels sprouts
1 lb chestnuts
1 oz butter
$\frac{3}{4}$ pint stock, or bouillon cube with water
pepper (ground from mill)

Method

Skin the chestnuts by blanching quickly in boiling water and peeling off skin while hot.

Wash and trim sprouts and cook in boiling salted water for 8-10 minutes, until tender, then drain.

Put chestnuts in a pan with half the butter and stock. Cover and cook until chestnuts are soft and the stock has been absorbed.

Meanwhile, put sprouts in a frying pan, add rest of butter in small pieces and shake pan gently until butter has melted, then add pepper.

Turn chestnuts into the pan and mix carefully with the sprouts. Put in a serving dish.

Brussels sprout cream

2 lb brussels sprouts
$\frac{1}{2}$ teacup hot milk
1 teacup of fresh white breadcrumbs
$1\frac{1}{2}$ oz butter
1 egg yolk
grated nutmeg (to taste)
salt and pepper

6-inch diameter cake tin, or ring mould (1 pint capacity)

Method

Wash and trim the sprouts, cook for 8-10 minutes or until tender in plenty of boiling salted water, then drain and rinse well in cold water. Drain again and press to remove any excess water. Pass through a Mouli sieve. Pour the hot milk on to the breadcrumbs in a bowl and leave to soak. Set oven at 350°F or Mark 4.

Put the sprout purée in a pan, add the butter, a small piece at a time, and stir over heat until the purée leaves the side of the pan. Draw aside, add soaked crumbs, egg yolk and nutmeg ; season well. Put purée into buttered tin or ring mould and cook au bain-marie in pre-set oven for 40 minutes. Leave for a few minutes before turning out.

The cream can be left quite plain or coated with $\frac{1}{2}$ pint white or cheese sauce.

Method of cooking cabbage

The most English — and most maligned — of all vegetables. To overcome this reputation every Cordon Bleu cook must remember the following golden rules :

1 Cabbage, like all vegetables that grow above the ground, must be put into plenty of boiling salted water and cooked uncovered.

2 Remove coarser outer leaves. Do not make a cut in stem base because this will spoil the shape and allow juices to escape. Wash well in several waters.

3 Avoid overcooking. For plain boiling, 10-12 minutes is enough. Although the cabbage must be tender, it should still have a certain bite and crispness. After draining, finish cooking in butter.

4 Avoid keeping cabbage hot for any length of time because this will give it an unpleasant smell and spoil the colour. Cook it early, by all means, but when tender tip into a colander, drain and rinse well with cold water. This will set the bright green colour. When the meal is nearly ready, turn the cabbage into a large shallow pan, heat quickly until steam stops rising, then add $\frac{1}{2}$-1 oz butter in small pieces and toss until melted. Season and serve.

Cabbage alsacienne

1 white Dutch cabbage (shredded)
1 oz butter
1 small head of celery (shredded)
1 wineglass dry white wine, or same quantity of stock with 1 teaspoon wine vinegar
salt and pepper
1 tablespoon chopped parsley

Method

Blanch cabbage in pan of boiling salted water for 1 minute, then drain well.

Melt butter in a shallow pan or casserole, add celery and cook for 2-3 minutes. Add the cabbage and wine, or stock and wine vinegar. Season well, cover and cook gently for 25-30 minutes. Sprinkle with chopped parsley before serving.

Braised cabbage

1 firm white cabbage
1 large onion
1 oz butter
1 cooking apple (peeled and sliced)
salt and pepper
1-2 tablespoons stock

Method

Cut the cabbage in quarters and cut away the core. Shred finely. If you are using hard white Dutch cabbage, blanch by putting into boiling, salted water for 1 minute, draining and refreshing with 1 cup of cold water. This is not necessary for green cabbage.

Slice the onion and put in a flameproof casserole with the butter. Cook over gentle heat until soft but not coloured. Add the cabbage to the pan with the peeled and sliced apple. Season, stir well and pour in the stock. Cover with non-stick (silicone) cooking paper and lid, and cook for 45-50 minutes on the bottom shelf of the oven, preset at 325°F or Mark 3.

Braised red cabbage

$1\frac{1}{2}$-2 lb red cabbage
1 onion
1 oz butter
2 cooking apples (peeled and sliced)
2-3 tablespoons wine vinegar
1 rounded tablespoon granulated sugar
salt and pepper
1 oz kneaded butter

Method

Wash and quarter the cabbage, cut out the stalk and shred finely. Put into a large pan of boiling water, cook for 1 minute only, then drain well. (The cabbage will turn a deep violet at this point but when the vinegar is added later it returns to its original colour.)

Slice the onion and cook in the butter in a flameproof casserole, until soft but not coloured. Peel and slice the apples, add to the onion and continue cooking for 2-3 minutes. Turn out on to a plate.

Add the cabbage to the casserole, layering with the apple mixture and sprinkling with the vinegar, 2-3 tablespoons water, sugar and seasoning. Cover with buttered paper and lid and cook in oven, pre-set at 325°F or Mark 3, for $1\frac{1}{2}$–2 hours. Stir from time to time and moisten with a little extra water, or stock, if necessary.

When very tender stir in the kneaded butter a small piece at a time, adding enough to bind the cabbage and juices. Adjust the seasoning.

This cabbage is even better cooked the day before and then reheated just before serving.

Stuffed cabbage pancakes

½ pint pancake batter

For filling
1 small, or ½ large, Dutch cabbage
1 onion (sliced)
1 oz butter
4 oz salt belly pork (cooked until tender and cut in strips), or unsmoked streaky bacon (cut in lardons and blanched)
4 tablespoons stock
salt and pepper

For mornay sauce
1 oz butter
1 rounded tablespoon plain flour
½ pint milk
2 oz cheese (grated)

Method

Prepare the batter and leave to stand in a cool place for 30 minutes. Fry pancakes and set aside.

Trim the cabbage, cut in four, discarding hard centre stalk, and shred finely. Put onion in a heavy flameproof casserole or pan with the butter, cover and cook slowly until soft. Add the pork or bacon to the pan and cook until golden-brown. Stir in the cabbage and stock, season to taste, cover with a buttered paper and a lid and cook slowly on top of the stove or in the oven at 350°F or Mark 4 until tender (for about 40 minutes). Prepare mornay sauce, reserving 1 tablespoon cheese.

Fill the pancakes with the cabbage mixture, fold them in half and place in a buttered ovenproof dish. Coat with mornay sauce, sprinkle with the reserved cheese and bake in oven, pre-set at 400°F or Mark 6, for 7-10 minutes or until golden-brown.

Dolmas

(with meat filling)

1 green cabbage
6 oz raw beef (minced)
1 small onion (finely chopped)
salt and pepper
5 tablespoons water
2 tablespoons rice (cooked)
plain flour
stock
1 bayleaf
½-¾ pint tomato sauce
chopped parsley

Method

Put onion into a bowl with the meat and seasoning. Work well together, adding the water gradually until the mixture is well beaten and pliable. Stir in rice and adjust seasoning.

Trim the cabbage, blanch it whole in boiling water for 2-3 minutes, drain well, then carefully detach the leaves, removing any hard stalk.

Put a small tablespoon of the mixture on each leaf, roll up like a parcel to form a sausage shape (see page 42). Then roll very lightly in flour and arrange in criss-cross layers in a thick pan or flameproof casserole. Barely cover with stock, bring carefully to the boil, season, add a bayleaf and simmer for 20-30 minutes on the stove, or in the oven pre-set at 350°F or Mark 4.

Meanwhile prepare a good, rather thin tomato sauce. Carefully lift the dolmas into ovenproof dish, draining well from the liquor, pour over the tomato sauce and cook in the oven at 350°F or Mark 4 for a further 20-30 minutes.

Sprinkle well with chopped parsley before serving.

Dolmas (with mushroom filling)

1 green cabbage
4 rounded tablespoons long grain rice
1 medium-size onion (finely chopped)
1 oz butter
4 oz mushrooms
2 hard-boiled eggs
1 dessertspoon plain flour
½ pint vegetable stock
1 dessertspoon tomato purée, or 1 tablespoon canned tomatoes
kneaded butter
½ lb tomatoes

Method

Boil rice for 10-12 minutes, or until tender in plenty of boiling salted water. Strain, rinse and strain again. Put on one side.

Wash cabbage, trim off stalk. Put into a large pan of boiling salted water and boil gently for 3-4 minutes. Lift out and begin peeling off the leaves. As soon as they become difficult to detach, put cabbage back into the boiling water to make the remainder soft and easy to remove. When all the leaves are detached, apart from the heart, prepare the filling.

To make filling : soften the onion in butter, add mushrooms, washed and finely chopped. Turn into a bowl and mix with the cooked rice and the hard-boiled eggs, finely chopped. Now snip out the cabbage stalk in each leaf with scissors. Place 1 dessertspoon of the mixture on each leaf and roll up like a small parcel. Roll each one lightly in flour, pack into a deep fireproof dish or pan.

Watchpoint Arrange each dolma at an angle so that it does not come into close contact with the others.

Pour over enough stock just to cover, bring to the boil, put on the lid, or cover with buttered paper, and simmer for about 45 minutes either on top of the stove or in the oven, pre-set at 325°F or Mark 3. Then tip stock into a pan, add either canned tomatoes or tomato purée, thicken with a little kneaded butter and boil again. Now peel fresh tomatoes, quarter and flick out seeds, then cut each quarter into three, lengthways. Arrange the dolmas in a serving dish or leave in the pan. Add tomato pieces to sauce and spoon over the dish.

How to stuff cabbage leaves for dolmas : take a softened leaf and spoon a little of the savoury filling into the centre. Fold leaf corners into the centre and roll up like a small parcel. Repeat this until all leaves are used. Then roll each of the finished leaves in a little flour

Cabbage Lorraine

1 firm cabbage
1 medium-size onion
2-3 tablespoons olive oil, or butter
4 large tomatoes (skinned, sliced and seeds removed)
salt and pepper
$\frac{1}{2}$ cup stock (optional)
1 carton (5 fl oz) soured cream, or yoghourt
1 tablespoon chopped parsley

Method

Trim and wash the cabbage thoroughly. Put it into a large pan of boiling, salted water and simmer for 4-5 minutes. Drain, refresh and drain again, pressing the cabbage lightly to extract any water. Then cut it in quarters, lengthways, remove some of the stalk if wished, tuck in the tips of the leaves and pack the quarters into an ovenproof dish or casserole.

Slice onion thinly, soften in pan with oil (or butter). Add the prepared tomatoes, season them well and cook until they are barely soft. Spoon tomato mixture over cabbage, cover casserole with buttered paper and a lid and cook gently in oven, pre-set at 350°F or Mark 4, for about 20-30 minutes or until the cabbage is tender. After the first 6-7 minutes add a little of the stock if necessary ; this will depend on the cabbage, since if it is really fresh the juice from the tomatoes is enough.

When cabbage is tender, spoon over the soured cream (or yoghourt), dust with the chopped parsley and return it to the oven for 1-2 minutes to reheat thoroughly.

Cabbage stuffed with chestnuts

1 firm green cabbage
1 lb chestnuts
1 onion (sliced)
1 oz butter
$1\frac{1}{4}$ pints jellied stock
about $\frac{1}{4}$ pint brown sauce

Method

Trim the cabbage, removing any damaged outside leaves, and plunge in boiling salted water for 5 minutes, tip into a colander and refresh with cold water. Remove the inner and outer shell of the chestnuts and put the nuts in a pan with the onion, butter and 1 pint of jellied stock ; cover and cook gently until the chestnuts are tender and the stock has evaporated.

Curl back the outer leaves of the cabbage, scoop out the centre and fill with the chestnuts. Reshape the cabbage and fit it into a buttered casserole, pour over $\frac{1}{4}$ pint of the stock, cover and cook in the oven, pre-set at 350°F or Mark 4, for 45-50 minutes. Spoon over the brown sauce and return to the oven for 5-10 minutes.

Chinese cabbage

This is a delicious vegetable.

Cook like ordinary cabbage, either quartered or shredded, and preferably with little or no water — for example, braised or as alsacienne (see pages 39 and 40).

Glazed carrots

1-2 lb carrots
1 teaspoon granulated sugar
1 oz butter
salt
mint (chopped)

Method

Peel, leave whole, or quarter if small. If very large, cut in thin slices. Put in a pan with water to cover, sugar, butter and a pinch of salt. Cover and cook steadily until tender, then remove lid and cook until all the water has evaporated, when the butter and sugar will form a glaze round the carrots.

Add a little chopped mint just before serving.

Carrots flamande

1 lb small even-size carrots (scraped)
½ oz butter
pinch of salt
1 teaspoon granulated sugar
½ pint water
12 oz peas (frozen)
sprig of mint
pepper (ground from mill)

Method

Put the scraped carrots in a pan with half the butter, salt and sugar. Add the water, cover and cook on fierce heat for about 20 minutes. Then add the peas, remaining butter and the mint and cook uncovered until carrots and peas are tender, by which time all the water should have disappeared.

Remove the mint, season with a little pepper and serve.

Carrots in poulette sauce

1 lb large carrots
½ oz butter
1 teaspoon granulated sugar

For 'quick' poulette sauce
1 oz butter
1 rounded tablespoon plain flour
¾ cup of vegetable, or chicken, stock
salt and pepper
5 tablespoons top of the milk
½ teaspoon lemon juice
1 large teaspoon chopped parsley

Method

Peel the carrots, cut them into thin rounds and put in a saucepan with the butter and sugar and cold water to cover. Cook them, covered, until tender (15-20 minutes).

To prepare poulette sauce: melt the butter, stir in the flour and cook over a low heat until a pale straw-colour. Draw pan aside, pour on the stock and blend until smooth. Return pan to the heat and stir until mixture begins to thicken, then season and add milk. Bring sauce to the boil and cook for another 2-3 minutes until syrupy in consistency. Draw pan aside and add the lemon juice and parsley.

Remove the lid from the pan of carrots, boil rapidly until all the water is driven off and the carrots are coated in a glaze of butter and sugar. Pour the sauce over the carrots and serve.

Cauliflower fritters

1 large cauliflower
1 bayleaf
¾ pint thick béchamel sauce (made with 2 oz butter, 2 oz flour and ¾ pint flavoured milk)
1 bunch of parsley
tomato sauce (for serving)

For fritter batter
¼ pint lukewarm water
1 tablespoon olive oil, or 1 oz butter (melted)
1 egg yolk
1 tablespoon double cream (optional)
4 oz plain flour
½ teaspoon salt
2 egg whites (stiffly whipped)

Deep fat bath

Method

Break the cauliflower into sprigs, retaining some of the stalk. Boil with the bayleaf in lightly salted water for 7-10 minutes, until barely cooked, then drain and allow to get cool. Prepare the béchamel sauce and cool on a plate.

To make the fritter batter stir the water, oil (or butter), egg yolk and cream (if used) into the flour and add the salt. Just before frying, fold in the egg whites.

Dip the cauliflower sprigs into the sauce when it is barely cold, making sure they are thickly coated. Put in refrigerator until really firm.

Heat the fat bath to 350-375°F, dip cauliflower into the batter, then drop carefully into the fat. Fry until a deep golden-brown, then drain on crumpled absorbent paper. Fry the parsley. Dish up, garnish with the parsley and serve tomato sauce separately.

Cauliflower with mustard mayonnaise

1 large cauliflower
1 carrot (grated)
½ pint mayonnaise
1 rounded teaspoon French mustard
salt and pepper
little creamy milk, or single cream (optional)
paprika pepper

Method

Wash cauliflower, break into sprigs and cook in boiling, salted water until barely tender (about 10 minutes). Drain and refresh. Dry sprigs thoroughly in absorbent paper or cloth, arrange in salad dish or bowl.

Grate carrot finely and fold into mayonnaise with mustard. If too thick, dilute with a little milk or cream. Spoon mayonnaise over cauliflower and dust with paprika pepper.

Cauliflower au gratin

1 large cauliflower
1 bayleaf
3 tablespoons grated cheese
3 tablespoons fresh white bread-crumbs
$\frac{1}{2}$ oz butter

For mornay sauce
$1\frac{1}{2}$ oz butter
3 tablespoons plain flour
$\frac{3}{4}$ pint milk
salt and pepper
3 tablespoons grated cheese
French, or English, mustard

When cooking cauliflower the addition of a bayleaf lessens the strong smell and gives a delicate flavour to the vegetable.

Method

Wash cauliflower thoroughly in salted water. Trim stalk but leave some green leaves on. Then break into sprigs (if necessary, use a knife to cut the stalk so that it remains attached to the sprigs and is not wasted) and boil for about 15 minutes, or until tender, in salted water with the bayleaf.

Meanwhile, prepare mornay sauce. Melt butter in a pan and stir in flour off the heat. Blend in milk, then stir until boiling. Cook for 2 minutes, season, draw on one side and cool before beating in the cheese by degrees. Then stir in the mustard to taste.

Watchpoint After mustard is added, do not boil the sauce because this will spoil the taste.

Now carefully drain cauliflower, butter a basin and arrange sprigs in it with the stalks towards the centre. When the basin is full, spoon in 2-3 tablespoons of sauce. Press down very lightly to bind the sprigs together and then invert the basin on to a fireproof dish. Take off basin, spoon sauce over and around, mix cheese and crumbs together and scatter over the cauliflower. Sprinkle well with melted butter and brown in the oven, pre-set at 400°F or Mark 6, for about 5 minutes.

Cauliflower with mushrooms

1 large cauliflower
1 tablespoon browned bread-crumbs
½ oz butter

For mushroom mixture
6-8 flat mushrooms
¾ pint milk, or ½ pint milk and ¼ pint water
1½-2 oz butter
2 tablespoons plain flour
salt and pepper

Method

Peel and stalk the mushrooms; wash the trimmings and simmer these in the milk, or milk and water mixture, in a covered pan for 30 minutes. Strain and reserve the liquid.

Boil cauliflower, head downwards. When the flower is tender, drain carefully and cut off superfluous stalk. Now place the cauliflower in an upright position in a fireproof dish.

To prepare the sauce: slice or quarter mushrooms and cook quickly for 4-5 minutes in ½ oz butter in a pan. Turn out on to a plate. Melt the remaining butter in the pan, stir in the flour off the heat and pour on the flavoured milk. Blend and stir until boiling. Season and cook for 2 minutes.

Take some of the sprigs from the centre of the cauliflower and set aside. Fill centre with the mushrooms and replace the sprigs. Carefully spoon the sauce over and round, scatter over the crumbs and add a little melted butter. Bake in the oven, pre-set at 400°F or Mark 6, for 10-15 minutes.

Cauliflower snow

(Choufleur à la neige)

1 large cauliflower
1 large onion (sliced)
2 oz butter
2 tomatoes (scalded, skinned and sliced)
1 oz plain flour
½ pint milk
salt and pepper
6 oz Cheddar cheese (grated)
4 eggs (separated)

Method

Cut cauliflower into sprigs and cook in boiling salted water, stems down, for 5-10 minutes. Sauté the onion in 1 oz butter until soft, add tomatoes and cook for 2-3 minutes.

Meanwhile make a white sauce with the remaining butter, and the flour and milk; season and add 4 oz of the cheese. Arrange cauliflower in a gratin dish, spoon over the onion and tomato mixture and coat with sauce.

Beat the egg whites stiffly and arrange on top of cauliflower, making four pockets for the egg yolks. Drop a yolk into each pocket. Sprinkle over the remaining cheese and grill until crisp and golden-brown.

Egg yolks are slipped into four pockets in the top of the beaten whites, then dusted with cheese

Cauliflower with almonds

1 large cauliflower
$1\frac{1}{2}$ oz almonds
4 tablespoons fresh white breadcrumbs
$1\frac{1}{2}$ oz butter
$\frac{1}{2}$ clove of garlic (very finely chopped) optional
salt and pepper

Method

Break cauliflower into large sprigs, leaving on some of the stalk and green leaf. Cook in a pan of boiling, salted water until tender (about 15 minutes). Meanwhile, blanch and shred almonds and soak in boiling water.

Drain the cooked cauliflower carefully. Butter a large basin, arrange cauliflower sprigs in this, stalks to the centre, cover with a small plate and press very lightly with the hand. Drain the almonds, dry well and mix with the breadcrumbs.

Heat the butter in a small pan and add the almond mixture and garlic ; stir over a steady heat until golden-brown, then season. Turn out the moulded cauliflower on to a hot serving dish and spoon over the almond and breadcrumb mixture.

This unusual combination of vegetables and nuts makes an appetising dish

Cauliflower cream

1 large cauliflower, or 2 small ones
1 bayleaf
handful of large spinach leaves
½ pint tomato sauce (for serving)

For panade
7½ fl oz béchamel sauce
salt and pepper
pinch of ground mace
2 eggs (one separated)
1 tablespoon cream

7-8 inch diameter deep sandwich tin, or 6-inch shallow cake tin

Method

Break the cauliflower into sprigs, using a little of the green and all of the stalk. Cook these until tender, with bayleaf, in a pan of boiling salted water. Drain cauliflower well, removing the bayleaf, and pass through a sieve. Return cauliflower to the pan with a knob of butter. Set it over low heat to dry to a fairly firm purée. Stir purée occasionally, then set aside.

Meanwhile grease the tin. Dip the spinach leaves in boiling water for a few seconds to make them pliable. Drain them well and line them into the tin with the shiny side of the leaf next to the tin.

Prepare the béchamel sauce (if not already made).

Add the cauliflower purée to the béchamel sauce, season well and add the mace ; beat in 1 whole egg and 1 yolk, reserving the white. Add the cream to sauce, whisk the white and fold it in. Turn cream at once into the prepared tin, cover it with buttered paper and steam or poach in a bain-marie on top of stove or in the oven, (pre-set at 325-350°F or Mark 3-4) for about 35-40 minutes, or until firm to the touch.

A few minutes before turning cream out, take it off the heat or remove it from the oven and allow it to stand. After turning out, spoon round a little tomato sauce and serve the rest separately.

Cauliflower soufflé with mornay sauce

1 medium-size cauliflower
browned breadcrumbs (for soufflé dish)
béchamel sauce (made with 1 oz butter, $\frac{3}{4}$ oz plain flour, $\frac{1}{4}$ pint flavoured milk)
3 egg yolks
4 egg whites
1 tablespoon grated Parmesan cheese (for dusting)

For mornay sauce
1 oz butter
$\frac{3}{4}$ oz plain flour
$\frac{1}{2}$ pint flavoured milk
2 oz grated cheese ($\frac{1}{2}$ Parmesan and $\frac{1}{2}$ Gruyère)

6-inch diameter top (No. 2 size) soufflé dish

Method

Set oven at 375°F or Mark 5. Butter the soufflé dish and dust with browned crumbs. To allow soufflé to rise above dish, tie round the outside a deep band of greaseproof paper to come 3 inches higher than dish.

Cut the cauliflower in four, removing the hard stalk ; cook in boiling salted water until quite tender (about 10 minutes). Drain well, refresh, and drain again, then rub cauliflower through a strainer (you should have 6 oz cauliflower purée).

Prepare the béchamel sauce and add the cauliflower purée to it. (Alternatively place béchamel sauce in a liquidiser, and add the cooked cauliflower a little at a time).

Beat the yolks into the cauliflower mixture one at a time. Whip the whites to a firm snow and fold into the mixture. Turn into the prepared soufflé dish, dust with the cheese, stand it on the centre shelf of the pre-set moderately hot oven and bake for about 20-25 minutes until well risen and brown. Meanwhile prepare the mornay sauce.

When cooked, the soufflé should be a little soft in the centre. Serve it immediately with the mornay sauce handed separately.

Braised celery

3 large sticks of celery
1 large onion
1 large carrot
1 oz butter
½ pint jellied stock
salt and pepper
bouquet garni

Method

Wash celery, split sticks in two, blanch in boiling, salted water and drain.

Dice the onion and carrot and sweat them in butter in a pan. Then add the celery, stock, seasoning and bouquet garni. Cover and braise for 1½ hours, or until tender, in oven pre-set at 325°F or Mark 3. Baste well from time to time.

When cooked, the gravy should be well reduced and the celery glazed. Dish up and strain gravy over the celery.

Sweetcorn fritters

1 cup of cooked frozen, or canned, sweetcorn kernels
2 eggs
salt and pepper
pinch of caster sugar
1 teaspoon baking powder
½-1 cup of fresh white breadcrumbs
oil (for frying)

Method

Separate the eggs, beat yolks well with the seasoning and sugar and then add the sweetcorn. Beat egg whites until stiff and fold into the sweetcorn with the baking powder and enough breadcrumbs to bring the mixture to a dropping consistency.

Heat the oil (enough to give a depth of ¼ inch in the frying pan), drop in sweetcorn mixture, a dessertspoon at a time, and fry until golden-brown on one side before turning and browning on the other side. Then lift out with a draining spoon and drain on crumpled absorbent paper.

Folding the stiffly beaten egg whites into the sweetoom mixture

Corn and cheese soufflé

For soufflé mixture
1 cup sweetcorn kernels (blanched)
2 tablespoons grated cheese (preferably Gruyère and Parmesan mixed)
1½ oz butter
1½ oz plain flour
good ½ pint milk (flavoured as for a béchamel)
2-3 tablespoons double cream
cayenne pepper
salt and pepper
4 egg yolks
5 egg whites
grated cheese (for dusting)

For mornay sauce
1¼ oz butter
1 oz plain flour
¾ pint milk
2-3 oz cheese (grated)
salt and pepper

7-inch diameter top (No. 1 size) soufflé dish

Method

Selt the oven at 375°F or Mark 5. Butter the soufflé dish and tie round a sheet of greaseproof paper so that it extends over top of dish by 3 inches (grease inside of this paper rim).

Melt the butter in a large pan, draw it aside and stir in the flour. Pour in the milk, blend and stir until boiling. Draw pan aside, beat in the cream, the well-drained corn, seasoning, cheese and the egg yolks, one at a time.

Whisk egg whites stiffly, cut and fold one large spoonful into the sauce, then add the remaining white in two parts. Continue to cut and fold but be careful not to overmix (as this expels air). Turn mixture into soufflé dish, dust the top with grated cheese, stand dish on a baking sheet and set in the centre of pre-set oven. Bake for 25-35 minutes.

Meanwhile prepare the mornay sauce. When soufflé is cooked, serve immediately with the mornay sauce handed separately.

Note : when entertaining it is an advantage to serve this sauce with a hot soufflé, especially if the soufflé has been too well baked through no fault of the cook, as it gives additional creaminess.

Corn-on-the-cob

This is known as 'green' corn and, for perfection, it should be eaten when the grain is milky-looking rather than a hard yellow. To test this, strip off a piece of the husk from the cob and have a look at the grains. Ideally the corn should be cooked within 30 minutes of picking ; if this is impossible, keep the cobs damp by covering with a cloth wrung out in cold water.

To cook, cut off the hard stalk at the base of the cob and strip off the husk. Rinse in cold water, then plunge cob into boiling unsalted water and cook for 7-8 minutes, then drain. **Note :** if the corn is not absolutely fresh, it will need to be cooked longer (ie. 15-25 minutes). Serve plain, with a dish of melted butter or with a knob of butter on each cob.

Corn is eaten off the cob, so finger bowls should be on the table. Special corn-on-the-cob holders can be bought to stick into each end of the cob, otherwise very small skewers or toothpicks can be used. Fresh corn is available in late summer. Frozen and canned cobs and kernels are obtainable all year round. These and canned creamed corn are all good as an accompaniment or as a base for many dishes.

Cooked corn-on-the-cob with a knob of butter melting on top

Courgette cream

$1\frac{1}{2}$ lb courgettes
6 oz cooked ham (half fat, half lean)
chopped parsley
4 eggs (separated)
scant 2 oz Gruyère cheese (grated)
salt and pepper
tomato sauce (for serving)

For béchamel sauce
1 oz butter
$\frac{3}{4}$ oz plain flour
good $\frac{1}{4}$ pint flavoured milk
salt and pepper

Charlotte tin, or ring mould ($1\frac{1}{2}$ pints capacity)

Method

Trim courgettes and slice them thinly, then boil in pan of salted water for 4-5 minutes. When barely tender, drain courgettes thoroughly, then mash. Chop ham and add to the courgettes with the parsley. Set oven at 400°F or Mark 6.

Make the béchamel sauce, stir in the egg yolks, then add the courgette mixture, cheese and seasoning. Whip egg whites firmly and fold into the mixture.

Turn the cream into the well greased tin (or mould) and cook in pre-set oven for about 25-30 minutes until well browned. Serve in the tin (or mould) or turn out, and pour round tomato sauce.

Buttered courgettes

7-8 courgettes (according to size)
$1\frac{1}{2}$ oz butter
1 tablespoon water
salt and pepper
$\frac{1}{2}$ tablespoon chopped parsley
$\frac{1}{2}$ tablespoon chopped fresh mixed herbs — optional

Method

Wipe and trim courgettes, blanch them if large and firm, otherwise put direct into a pan or a flameproof casserole with butter and 1 tablespoon of water.

Add seasoning and press buttered paper on top ; cover with a lid (to conserve all juices). Cook slowly on top of stove for 15-20 minutes, or until tender. Spinkle with parsley, and other herbs if wished.

Courgettes maison

8 small courgettes
4 tomatoes
1 oz butter
1 shallot (finely chopped)
1 teaspoon paprika pepper
salt and pepper
½ lb shelled prawns
1 tablespoon grated Parmesan cheese (for dusting)

For mornay sauce
1 oz butter
1 oz plain flour
½ pint milk
2 oz Parmesan cheese (grated)

Method

Trim each end of the courgettes, cook whole for 5 minutes in boiling salted water, then drain and refresh them. Remove a thin slice lengthways from each courgette, carefully scoop out the flesh with the point of a teaspoon and chop it. Scald and skin the tomatoes ; cut in four, discard the seeds and chop flesh coarsely.

Melt the butter in a saucepan, add the chopped shallot and cook, covered, until quite soft but not brown ; add the paprika, chopped courgette flesh and tomatoes. Season and cook briskly for 2-3 minutes. Stir in the prawns.

Put the courgette cases in a buttered gratin dish and fill them with the tomato and prawn mixture. Prepare mornay sauce and spoon it over the courgettes ; dust with cheese. Brown in oven at 425°F or Mark 7 for 10-12 minutes.

1

2

1 *Slicing the cooked courgettes lengthways and scooping out the flesh*
2 *Filling courgette cases with the prawn and tomato mixture before coating them with mornay sauce and grated cheese and browning*

Courgettes maison make an appetising starter for a dinner party

Courgettes au gratin

1 lb courgettes
$\frac{1}{2}$ teaspoon salt
$\frac{1}{4}$ pint water
1 egg
1 small carton ($2\frac{1}{2}$ fl oz) double cream
2 rounded tablespoons grated Gruyère cheese
black pepper (ground from mill)
$\frac{1}{2}$ oz butter

Method

Wipe courgettes, trim the ends, cut in slanting $\frac{1}{2}$-inch slices and put in a sauté pan with the salt and water. Cover pan and cook over moderate heat until water has almost evaporated.

Mix the egg, cream and cheese together, reserving 1 tablespoon of cheese, and season with black pepper.

Slide courgettes carefully into ovenproof gratin dish. Pour over the creamy mixture and sprinkle with the reserved cheese. Dot the top with shavings of butter and bake in oven, pre-set at 400°F or Mark 6, for about 10 minutes or until just set and golden-brown.

Courgette salad

1 lb small courgettes
2 shallots (finely chopped)
4 tablespoons olive oil
1 dessertspoon paprika pepper
salt and pepper
little caster sugar
1 teaspoon dill seeds, or a little fresh dill (chopped)
2 tablespoons wine vinegar

Serve with cold roast beef or lamb, or as part of an hors d'œuvre.

Method

Wipe the courgettes and slice thinly. Heat the oil in a deep frying, or sauté, pan (taking care not to get the oil too hot) then add the chopped shallots and the courgettes. Sauté slowly until the courgettes are partially cooked, then add the paprika, seasoning, sugar, dill and vinegar. Continue to cook, turning frequently, for a further 5 minutes or until tender. Adjust seasoning and turn out to cool.

Sauté cucumber

1 large cucumber
$\frac{1}{2}$-1 oz butter
1 bunch spring onions (trimmed), or 1 small onion (chopped)
salt and pepper
fresh mint (chopped) — to garnish

Method

Peel cucumber, using a stainless steel knife ; split in four lengthways. Cut across into 1-inch chunks, blanch in boiling, salted water for 1 minute, then drain well.

Melt butter in a pan, add spring onions (or chopped onion). Cover and cook for 1 minute. Add cucumber and season. Cover and cook for 5-6 minutes or until just tender, occasionally shaking the pan gently. Garnish with fresh mint.

Watchpoint Do not overcook or cucumber will become watery and tasteless.

Sweet and sour cucumber

1 large cucumber
salt
1 tablespoon caster sugar
1 tablespoon wine vinegar
black pepper (ground from mill)
lemon juice (to taste)
chopped mint (to garnish)

Method

Peel the cucumber, split it in half lengthways and then cut in slices ; sprinkle with salt, cover with a plate and set in the refrigerator for 30 minutes.

Meanwhile mix the sugar and vinegar together. On removing the cucumber from the refrigerator, drain off any liquid and add it to the sugar and vinegar ; stir until the sugar has dissolved. Add black pepper and lemon juice to taste. Pour this liquid over the cucumber and garnish with mint before serving.

Cucumber Vichy

1 large cucumber
½ lb new carrots
½ oz butter
1 teaspoon granulated sugar
large pinch of salt
1 dessertspoon chopped parsley
pepper (ground from mill)

Method

Peel the cucumber, cut in half lengthways and then across in ½-inch slices. Blanch in boiling salted water for 1 minute, then drain, refresh and set aside. Peel and quarter carrots and put in a pan with the butter, sugar, salt and enough water to cover. Cook until just tender (about 10 minutes) with the lid on.

Take lid off the pan and continue cooking until the water has evaporated ; add the prepared cucumber and parsley and season with pepper. Toss vegetables carefully until they are coated with the butter, sugar and parsley glaze.

Tossing the blanched cucumber with the cooked carrots in the pan to coat them with butter, sugar and parsley

Sweet cucumber pickle

5 lb ridge cucumbers (weighed when peeled and sliced)
1½ lb small onions
2 green peppers
2 oz salt

For pickle
1 lb granulated, or demerara, sugar
2 oz mustard seed
2 teaspoons celery seed
1 dessertspoon turmeric
1 teaspoon ground mace
scant 1¾ pints white malt, or white wine, vinegar

Method

Slice the onions finely, cut the peppers in half, remove the seeds and shred flesh. Layer the vegetables (including cucumbers) in a bowl and sprinkle well with salt. Cover and leave for 2-3 hours. Then turn into a colander, rinse with cold water and drain.

Put all the ingredients for the pickle into a shallow stewpan, or preserving pan, and stir well ; bring to the boil. Boil for 3 minutes. Draw aside, add the vegetables and shake the pan well to mix thoroughly. Bring back to boiling point, stirring from time to time to make sure that all the vegetables are covered with the boiling liquid. Then draw aside, cool and turn into jars. Cover with vegetable parchment or use jars with screw-tops.

Buttered chicory

4-5 large heads of chicory
½ oz butter
salt and pepper
juice of ½ lemon
2 tablespoons water
chopped parsley — to garnish

Method

Rub butter over the bottom of a shallow pan or deep frying pan. Peel off one or two outer leaves of chicory, if necessary; trim the bottoms and wipe the heads. Cut into 1-inch thick diagonal slices, put into pan with seasoning, lemon juice and water.

Press a piece of buttered paper or foil on top, cover pan and cook on low heat for 7-8 minutes until chicory is tender, shaking pan occasionally. Finish off with a little chopped parsley.

Chicory ardennaise

5 good heads of chicory
2-3 tablespoons water
squeeze of lemon juice
2 oz lean cooked ham (cut in julienne strips)
little grated cheese and melted butter (for browning)

For mornay sauce
good ½ oz butter
scant ½ oz plain flour
½ pint milk
1½ oz grated cheese (Gruyère and Parmesan mixed, or dry Cheddar)
½ teaspoon French, or made English, mustard
salt and pepper

This recipe gets its name from the Belgian region of the Ardennes, famed for its ham. However, the ham in this recipe doesn't have to be ardennaise — any good lean ham may be used.

Method

Set oven at 350°F or Mark 4. Trim the chicory, put into a well-buttered flameproof casserole with the water and lemon juice. Cover with a piece of buttered paper and the lid. Set on low heat for 5-6 minutes, then put in the pre-set oven for 45-50 minutes, until the chicory is clear-looking and very tender.

Meanwhile prepare sauce and stir the ham into it. Lift the chicory on to a serving dish, coat with the sauce, dust well with the grated cheese, sprinkle with melted butter and brown it under the grill.

Braised chicory

6-8 pieces of chicory
1 oz butter
juice of $\frac{1}{2}$ lemon
$\frac{1}{2}$ teaspoon salt (dissolved in 1 tablespoon water)
black pepper (ground from mill)

Method

Wipe the chicory, remove any marked outside leaves and scoop out the small core at the bottom. Rub the butter round a casserole dish, put in the chicory and pour over it the lemon juice and salt water.

Add a little black pepper, cover with a buttered greaseproof paper and the lid of the casserole and cook for 1 hour in oven pre-set at 350°F or Mark 4.

Braised chicory with orange

1 lb chicory
1-2 oz butter
salt
pepper (ground from mill)
rind and juice of 1 orange

Method

Wipe the chicory, remove any damaged outer leaves and scoop out the core at the bottom.

Butter a casserole, put in the chicory, season and add the rind and juice of the orange. Cover with a buttered paper and lid and cook in oven, pre-set at 350°F or Mark 4, for about $1\frac{1}{2}$ hours.

Florence fennel (finocchio)

This is more commonly known as a salad, but when cooked as a vegetable it loses some of its strong-tasting qualities. It is imported to Britain because it is difficult to grow here, and is available in early summer and sometimes throughout the year. It has thick, fleshy white bulbs, crisp and juicy and tasting of aniseed. They are delicious sliced raw in a salad, or quartered, plainly boiled, tossed in butter and served as a special vegetable.

Finocchio 'en coquilles'

2 large heads of fennel
¼ oz butter
grated Gruyère cheese (for dusting)

For béchamel sauce
good ½ oz butter
good ½ oz plain flour
½ pint flavoured milk
1-2 tablespoons cream

4-6 large scallop shells

Method

Quarter the fennel, or if it is large, cut each one into 8 pieces. Plunge fennel into salted boiling water and simmer for 6-7 minutes or until tender. Drain fennel, return it to the pan with ¼ oz butter.

Prepare the béchamel sauce, finishing with the cream. Well butter the scallop shells, put a spoonful of sauce in each one, then arrange the fennel in them ; coat with the rest of the sauce, give a light dusting of Gruyère cheese and brown in the oven, pre-set at 400°F or Mark 6, for 6-7 minutes. Serve this dish hot.

Fennel and lemon salad

2-3 heads of fennel (according to size)
2 ripe thin-skinned lemons

For dressing
juice of extra ½ lemon
3 tablespoons oil
salt and pepper
sugar (to taste)
1 tablespoon roughly chopped parsley

Method

Slice the fennel finely and put into a bowl. Pare 2-3 strips of rind from 1 lemon and cut this rind into shreds, then blanch, drain and refresh it and set aside. Slice away the peel and white pith from both lemons and cut out the flesh from between the membranes with a sharp knife, holding the lemon in one hand so that eventually only the membranes are left in your hand. Add the lemon segments to the fennel.

To make dressing : squeeze the membranes left from the two lemons to get out any juice and, if necessary, make up to a good tablespoon with some of the juice from the extra ½ lemon. Beat in the oil and season well. Make the dressing rather sweet, especially if the lemons are not really ripe. Add it to the fennel and lemon with 1 tablespoon of the chopped parsley. Toss well and serve scattered with the blanched lemon rind.

Sauté finocchio

3 heads of fennel
2½ oz butter
salt and pepper
rind and juice of ½ lemon
1 rounded tablespoon chopped mixed herbs, or parsley

Method

Slice fennel thickly ; melt two-thirds of the butter in a sauté or deep frying pan, put in fennel, season, cover pan and cook gently, shaking the pan occasionally, for 5-6 minutes. Remove pan lid, increase the heat and continue to cook fennel for a further 2-3 minutes (this is to dry off any surplus moisture). Turn fennel into a hot serving dish.

Wipe out pan, drop in the remaining butter and cook it to a noisette (ie. until it turns a good brown) ; then add lemon rind and juice with the herbs. Pour this butter, while still foaming, over the fennel and serve.

An unusual accompanying vegetable — sauté finocchio with noisette butter

Leek and egg salad

4-5 leeks (according to size)
salt
little French dressing
3 hard-boiled eggs
$\frac{1}{4}$-$\frac{1}{2}$ pint mayonnaise
paprika pepper

Method

Wash the leeks thoroughly. Split in half lengthways and tie together to form a neat bundle. Boil in salted water until just tender (about 12 minutes), drain and refresh. Untie, put in dish and pour over a little French dressing.

Cut white of eggs into strips and scatter over the leeks. Sieve yolks through a wire bowl strainer. Thin the mayonnaise, if necessary, with 1 tablespoon of boiling water. Spoon this over the salad to coat leeks, and sprinkle sieved yolks on top. Dust with paprika pepper and serve lightly chilled.

Leeks vinaigrette

6-8 small leeks
$1\frac{1}{2}$ oz currants (soaked for 1 hour in boiling water)
2 tablespoons fresh tomato pulp, or 1 tablespoon tomato purée diluted with 1 tablespoon water
2 tablespoons red wine vinegar
4-5 tablespoons oil
salt and pepper
sugar (to taste)

Method

Wash the leeks thoroughly and cook them in boiling salted water for 7-10 minutes, then drain, refresh and drain again. Drain and dry the soaked currants. Put the tomato pulp (or diluted purée) into a basin with the vinegar, oil and seasoning, mix together and sweeten to taste with the sugar ; add the currants.

Split the leeks lengthways and arrange in a dish. Spoon dressing over the leeks and chill slightly. Serve as a starter with hot fresh rolls and butter.

Currants have been added to the dressing which is spooned over the leeks. The dish is chilled before being served

Leek and bacon pie

12 oz quantity of puff pastry

For filling
10 leeks
10 oz green streaky bacon
3 eggs
$\frac{1}{2}$ pint chicken, or veal, stock
salt and pepper
4-5 tablespoons single cream, or creamy milk
1 egg (beaten)

$8\frac{1}{2}$*-9 inch diameter pie plate*

Method

First prepare the filling : trim the leeks, wash them well and cut into $\frac{3}{4}$-1 inch diagonal slices. Put these into a pan of boiling salted water, boil gently for 4-5 minutes, then drain them very well.

Remove any rind and rust from the bacon and cut into lardons. Put them in a pan with the water, bring to the boil, drain, rinse and drain them again.

Break the eggs into a bowl, beat with a fork, season and add the cream (or milk). Add the leeks and bacon, moisten with stock and set aside. Set the oven at 400°F or Mark 6.

Take about half of the pastry, roll it out very thinly and line into the pie plate, making sure that it overlaps the edge slightly. Prick the bottom with a fork and turn the leek mixture into this. Roll out the other half of the pastry to about $\frac{1}{4}$ inch thick, cover the pie with it, press down around the edges and trim. Mark the top of the pastry with the back of the knife, roll out the trimmings and make either leaves, rose or tassel for decoration.

Scallop the edge of the pie with your fingers, brush over with the beaten egg, chill for 5-10 minutes, then bake in pre-set oven for about 25 minutes or until pastry is a good russet-brown and well risen. Serve hot.

Watchpoint Before baking put a baking sheet into the oven for a few minutes to get thoroughly hot. Then set the pie plate on this so that the bottom of the tart will be well cooked from the additional heat from the baking sheet.

Braised leeks

6 leeks
1 oz butter

Method

Trim the leeks, make a cross cut in the top and wash thoroughly under running water. Blanch by putting into boiling, salted water for 1 minute. Drain well. Put in a well-buttered casserole, cover tightly and cook for 45-50 minutes on the bottom shelf of the oven, pre-set at 325°F or Mark 3.

Lentil purée

6 oz Egyptian lentils
1 onion (stuck with clove)
1 carrot (cut in rounds)
salt and pepper
bouquet garni
stock (optional)
2 oz butter
celery

This is an excellent accompaniment to casseroled rabbit. Dried peas can be used instead of the Egyptian lentils.

Method

Soak lentils overnight. Then drain, cook in plenty of water brought slowly to boil, with onion, carrot, bouquet garni and a little salt. Simmer until tender.

Sieve lentil mixture, lighten with stock if it is too thick, draw aside from heat and beat in butter with a little pepper.

Before serving, stir into purée a little raw, chopped celery.

Dahl

6 oz Masoor lentils
1 oz butter
1 small onion (finely chopped)
½ teaspoon ground turmeric
1 teaspoon garam masala
1 pint good stock
1 teaspoon salt

This is a traditional accompaniment to curry.

Method

Cover lentils with cold water and soak for 1 hour. Melt the butter in a pan, add the chopped onion, the drained lentils, spices and stock. Cover and cook gently for 50 minutes. Add a little salt and continue cooking until the lentils are quite soft. The consistency should be that of thick pea soup. Taste for salt and add more if necessary.

Garam masala

¾ oz cinnamon
¼ oz cloves
¾ oz brown cardamom seeds
¼ oz black cumin seeds
good pinch of mace
good pinch of nutmeg

Method

Grind ingredients together, or pound in a mortar, then pass through a fine sieve. This will keep up to two weeks in an airtight container.

Lentil cutlets

4 oz Egyptian lentils
½ oz fat
½ oz plain flour
¼ pint milk, or stock
4 oz white breadcrumbs
1 onion (finely chopped)
little lemon juice
1 teaspoon salt
good pinch of pepper
½ teaspoon mixed herbs
1 egg (beaten) — for coating
dry breadcrumbs (for coating)
fat (for frying)

Method

Soak lentils overnight and drain. Then put in plenty of lightly salted water, bring to the boil and simmer until tender.

Make a thick white sauce with the fat, flour and milk (or stock), add all the other ingredients (except those for coating), mix well and turn on to a wet plate to cool. Form into cutlet shapes or rissoles and coat with egg and breadcrumbs. Fry until golden-brown and serve hot.

Lentil salad

6 oz Egyptian lentils
1 onion (stuck with clove)
1 onion (cut in rounds)
salt
bouquet garni
stock (optional)
1 clove of garlic (crushed with ½ teaspoon salt)
4-6 tablespoons French dressing
pepper (ground from mill)
6-8 pickling onions
½ lb tomatoes
1 head of celery
1 lemon

This salad can be served with pork, cold roast chicken and game.

Method

Soak lentils overnight ; then drain, and cook in plenty of slightly salted water (brought slowly to the boil) with onion, carrot and bouquet garni. Simmer until tender and drain. Remove bouquet garni and sieve lentil mixture ; lighten with stock if it is too thick and allow to cool. Add the crushed garlic and French dressing to the purée and season very well, adding plenty of ground black pepper.

Slice the pickling onions, scald and skin the tomatoes, remove the core at the top, squeeze out the seeds and chop tomatoes roughly. Mix the pickling onions and tomatoes into purée and pile into a serving dish. Surround with curled celery and lemon quarters.

Buttered marrow

1 marrow
1-2 oz butter
salt and pepper
chopped parsley

Method

Peel the marrow, remove seeds and cut into 2-inch squares. Melt butter in a large shallow pan and add marrow. Season and cover with buttered paper and a lid. Cook over gentle heat until tender, shaking the pan from time to time. Allow 15-20 minutes cooking time and garnish with chopped parsley.

Stuffed marrow 1

2 small marrows, or 1 large one
2 oz butter (melted)
scant $\frac{1}{2}$ pint béchamel sauce (made with 1 oz butter, 1 oz flour, $\frac{1}{2}$ pint flavoured milk, 2 tablespoons cream - optional)
$\frac{1}{2}$-$\frac{3}{4}$ lb small French, or runner, beans
2-3 tomatoes
$\frac{1}{2}$ pint tomato sauce (made with vegetable stock)
3-4 hard-boiled eggs

Note : any other seasonal vegetable can be used in place of the beans. If wished, the béchamel sauce can be flavoured with onion.

Method

Set oven at 350°F or Mark 4.

Peel the marrow, cut in half, scooping out seeds, and blanch in boiling water for 2-3 minutes. Lift out carefully with a slice and drain and dry on absorbent paper. Set in a baking dish and brush well with melted butter inside the marrow and outside. Season, and cover with a piece of foil, or well buttered paper. Put into pre-set moderate oven and cook for 15-20 minutes or until the marrow is just tender. After 10 minutes remove the paper and baste with some more of the melted butter.

Meanwhile prepare béchamel sauce. Trim French beans, or cut the runner beans into diamonds, and cook in plenty of boiling salted water until tender. Drain, and finish with a little of the melted butter ; set aside. Scald, skin and quarter the tomatoes, flick out the seeds and cut flesh into coarse shreds. Add shreds to the prepared tomato sauce and put aside to keep hot. Chop the hard-boiled eggs and mix into the béchamel sauce. The mixture should be really thick and creamy.

When the marrows are tender, bring the tomato sauce up to the boil and pour it into a large oval serving dish. Set the marrow in this and fill two halves with the egg mixture and the other two with beans. Put back in the oven for a few minutes, if necessary, to make thoroughly hot. Serve for a lunch, or supper, dish.

Stuffed marrow 2

1 medium-size marrow
1 large onion (finely chopped)
2 oz beef dripping
1 rounded tablespoon plain flour
about $\frac{3}{4}$ lb cooked beef, or lamb, or veal (minced or cut in fine dice)
$\frac{1}{2}$-1 cup stock
salt and pepper
knob of butter (optional)
fruit sauce, or ketchup (optional)
$\frac{1}{2}$ pint tomato sauce
chopped herbs, or parsley (to garnish)

Method

Set oven at 350°F or Mark 4.

Peel the marrow, split it in two lenghtways and scoop out the seeds with a metal spoon. Blanch the halves by plunging them into boiling salted water in a large pan and simmer for 2-3 minutes. Drain thoroughly.

Brown the onion in about half the dripping then draw aside, stir in the flour and add the meat. Moisten with about $\frac{1}{2}$ cup of stock and stir until just at boiling point. Draw pan aside. Season and, if wished, add knob of butter and fruit sauce (or ketchup).

Watchpoint The meat mixture should be nicely moist but not too soft.

Fill the marrow halves with this mixture and reshape ; tie with tape or string. Heat the rest of the dripping in a deep pan, or ovenproof dish, or roasting tin, put in the marrow, baste and moisten with any remaining stock. Cover the marrow with a piece of foil, or greaseproof paper, and put in pre-set moderate oven. Cook for about 20-30 minutes, then remove the paper and baste well. Put back into the oven for a further 30 minutes, or until marrow is tender, basting occasionally. The marrow should brown nicely.

Sieve and strain the liquid into a pan with $\frac{1}{2}$ pint tomato sauce and boil this up. Remove the tape or string and spoon a little of the sauce over the marrow. Serve the rest of the sauce separately. Sprinkle with chopped herbs or parsley.

Hungarian marrow

1 small young marrow
1-2 oz butter
1 dessertspoon paprika pepper
1 small onion (finely chopped)
2-3 tablespoons wine vinegar
about 6 dill, or caraway, seeds
1 teaspoon caster sugar
kneaded butter

Method

Peel marrow, cut into quarters, scoop out seeds and slice thinly. Melt 1-2 oz butter in a large pan. Put in the marrow and fry quickly for 4-5 minutes, shaking the pan well. Add the paprika. Take out the marrow and put in the onion, with more butter if necessary.

Cover the pan for 1-2 minutes to cook the onion, then add the vinegar, dill (or caraway) seeds and the sugar. Thicken slightly with kneaded butter, replace the marrow, cover and simmer for 5 minutes, by which time it should be just tender.

Stuffed mushrooms

2 large mushrooms per person, and 2-3 over
½ oz butter
1 teaspoon onion (chopped)
1 tablespoon fresh white bread-crumbs, or slice of crust soaked in milk
salt and pepper
1 teaspoon chopped parsley
pinch of dried mixed herbs

Method

Cup mushrooms are best for this dish. Wash and peel them, then cut across the stalks level with the caps. Chop the trimmings with the extra mushrooms. Cook for 1-2 minutes in the butter with the chopped onion. Add the crumbs (or soaked crust, squeezed and broken up with a fork). Season and add herbs.

Spread this mixture on to the mushrooms, dot with butter and set them on a baking sheet, or in an ovenproof dish. Bake for 12-15 minutes in oven, pre-set at 400°F or Mark 7, and serve in an ovenproof dish.

Mushrooms au gratin

1 lb mushrooms
1-½ oz butter
salt and pepper
pinch of mace
cayenne pepper
2-3 tablespoons browned breadcrumbs
2-3 tablespoons grated Parmesan cheese

For sauce
1 oz butter
1 oz plain flour
7½ fl oz milk
2½ fl oz double cream

Method

Trim, wash and dry mushrooms (leaving on stalks), and fry briskly in the butter. Turn into a gratin dish, season with salt, pepper, mace and a sprinkling of cayenne.

To make sauce, melt butter in a pan, stir in flour off the heat and blend in the milk. Stir over heat until boiling, boil for 1 minute, then add the cream. Spoon sauce over mushrooms, dust with 2-3 tablespoons browned crumbs, 2-3 tablespoons Parmesan cheese, and bake in oven, pre-set at 400°F or Mark 6, for 7-10 minutes.

Casserole of mushrooms and potatoes

1 ½ lb even-size potatoes, or 1 lb new potatoes
8 oz button mushrooms
1 oz butter
2 tablespoons plain flour
1 pint milk, or ½ pint milk and ½ pint potato water
salt and pepper
1-2 tablespoons double cream (or milk and potato water)
pinch of grated nutmeg

Method

Peel potatoes and cut each one in four. (If using new ones, leave them whole.) Trim the cut edges with a potato peeler. Cook carefully in salted water until barely tender. Tip away water (if not using), dry over gentle heat. Cover and set aside.

Wash the mushrooms in salted water and trim the stalks.

Watchpoint Be careful not to pull out the stalks or the mushrooms will shrink during cooking. The stalk keeps the mushroom in shape.

Melt the butter and toss mushrooms in it over a high heat. Mix in the flour, milk (or milk and potato water) and seasoning and stir until boiling. Add the potatoes, cover the pan and simmer for 10 minutes. Stir in cream and a pinch of grated nutmeg.

Note : this dish is best done with tiny, new potatoes but canned new ones will do. In this case, follow the instructions for heating on the can. Drain and put them into the sauce. Do **not** simmer for 10 minutes as with fresh potatoes, but finish off immediately with the cream and nutmeg and keep warm.

Mushroom soufflé

8 oz flat mushrooms, or mushroom stalks (finely chopped)
1 oz butter
1 tablespoon freshly chopped mixed herbs (parsley, mint, chives)
salt and pepper
4 egg yolks
5 egg whites
1 tablespoon grated cheese
1 tablespoon browned breadcrumbs

For béchamel sauce
$1\frac{1}{2}$ oz butter
1 rounded tablespoon plain flour
$\frac{1}{2}$ pint milk (infused with 1 slice onion, $\frac{1}{2}$ bayleaf, 6 peppercorns, 1 blade of mace, a few pieces of carrot)

7-inch diameter top (size No. 1) soufflé dish

Method

Tie a band of greaseproof paper round soufflé dish so that it comes 3 inches above rim ; butter inside. Set oven at 375°F or Mark 5.

Wash mushrooms but do not peel, chop them finely. Cook in 1 oz butter in a fairly large pan for 4-5 minutes. Increase heat, if necessary, to drive off any excess liquid. Add herbs and seasoning. Prepare béchamel sauce and stir into the mushroom mixture.

Beat egg yolks into the béchamel and mushroom mixture, one at a time. Whip whites to a firm snow, cut and stir 1 tablespoon of these into the mixture, using a metal spoon. Then stir in remainder.

Turn into the prepared dish. Sprinkle top with cheese and browned crumbs mixed together and bake for 25-30 minutes in pre-set oven.

Mushroom and egg à la crème

3 oz mushrooms (sliced)
$\frac{1}{2}$ oz butter
squeeze of lemon juice
$\frac{1}{4}$ pint double cream
5-6 eggs
salt and pepper
pinch of grated nutmeg
3 oz Gruyère cheese (grated)

5-6 ramekins

This makes a very good party dish.

Method

Set oven at 350°F or Mark 4. Cook the sliced mushrooms very quickly in the butter with a squeeze of lemon. Pour half the cream into the ramekins, break the eggs carefully on top and then cover with the mushrooms.

Season the remaining cream, add grated nutmeg, and spoon it over the mushrooms. Cover each ramekin with a thick layer of grated Gruyère cheese, stand in a bain-marie of very hot water and cook in pre-set oven for 10 minutes. Serve hot.

Mushroom and egg bouchées

8 oz quantity of puff pastry
egg wash (made with 1 egg beaten with $\frac{1}{2}$ teaspoon salt)

For filling
$\frac{1}{4}$ lb mushrooms (quartered, or sliced)
4 eggs (hard-boiled and coarsely chopped)
$1\frac{1}{2}$ oz butter
1 rounded tablespoon plain flour
$\frac{1}{2}$ pint milk (infused with 1 slice of onion, $\frac{1}{2}$ bayleaf, 6 peppercorns
salt and pepper

$2\frac{1}{2}$-inch diameter fluted cutter, $1\frac{1}{2}$-inch diameter cutter (fluted, or plain)

The bouchée cases can be made the same day or a few days beforehand and stored in an airtight container. This filling is sufficient for 6-8 bouchées.

Method

Set oven at 425°F or Mark 7. Roll out pastry to just over $\frac{1}{4}$ inch thick and stamp it out into bouchées $2\frac{1}{2}$ inches in diameter. Set on a dampened baking sheet and brush with egg wash. Make circular incisions with the smaller cutter to form lids. Bake in pre-set oven for 15-20 minutes until golden-brown.

Trim mushrooms, wash them quickly, drain, and quarter or slice them depending on their size. Melt half the butter, add the mushrooms and sauté them for 2-3 minutes. Draw pan off the heat and add the remaining butter (the heat of the pan will melt it automatically) and blend in the flour and strained, flavoured milk. Season and stir sauce until boiling; cook for 2-3 minutes, then add the eggs.

Remove lids and fill bouchées with the mixture. Replace lids and reheat for a few minutes in oven before serving very hot.

If you have baked bouchées a few days before, the best way to reheat them is as follows: first set oven at 350°F or Mark 4. Fill *cold* bouchées with hot filling and heat for 10 minutes.

Mushroom omelet

3 oz mushrooms (sliced or quartered)
$\frac{1}{4}$ oz butter
2 rounded teaspoons plain flour
3-4 tablespoons stock, or water
salt and pepper
squeeze of lemon juice
4 - egg omelet

Method

Slice or quarter mushrooms, sauté for 2-3 minutes in butter in a pan. Stir in flour, add liquid and seasoning, stir until boiling. Then add lemon juice. The consistency should be creamy. Make a plain omelet, pour in mushroom mixture before folding omelet over.

Mushroom beignets

¾ lb firm button mushrooms
fritter batter
deep fat (for frying)
fried parsley (to garnish)

For devil sauce dip
½ pint mayonnaise, or boiled dressing
1 tablespoon finely chopped pickles
1 tablespoon finely chopped parsley
1 clove of garlic (crushed)
1 teaspoon grated onion
1 tablespoon chopped capers
1 tablespoon chopped olives
salt and pepper

Method

Trim the stalks of the mushrooms, wash quickly in salted water and dry well.

Prepare the fritter batter, cover and stand in a warm place for 30-40 minutes.

Combine ingredients for dip and season well. Dip each mushroom into the batter and fry in deep fat. Drain on absorbent paper and serve on cocktail sticks. Garnish with fried parsley and hand devil sauce dip separately.

Mushroom tartlets

4 oz quantity of shortcrust pastry
½ lb firm mushrooms
1-2 oz butter (to sauté)
salt and pepper
1 tablespoon tomato chutney
dash of Tabasco sauce
2 oz anchovy butter

8-9 tartlet tins

Method

Prepare the pastry, line tartlet tins and bake blind. Leave to cool, then turn out.

Slice the mushrooms thickly and sauté in the butter. Season well, add chutney and Tabasco.

Put a spoonful of the hot mushroom mixture in each pastry case. Just before serving put a pat of anchovy butter on top of each tartlet.

Mushroom flan

For shortcrust pastry
6 oz plain flour
pinch of salt
2 oz butter
2 oz shortening
2 tablespoons cold water

For filling
$\frac{1}{2}$ pint milk
1 blade mace
1 bayleaf
6 peppercorns
$1\frac{1}{2}$ oz butter
1 medium-size onion (thinly sliced)
6 oz mushrooms (sliced)
3 tablespoons plain flour
salt and pepper
2 tablespoons double cream (optional)
1 egg yolk
1 small egg

7-inch diameter flan ring

Method

Make the shortcrust pastry and line on to the flan ring, reserving about one-third to cut into strips for the top. Set aside to chill. Set oven at 400°F or Mark 6.

Infuse the milk with the mace, bayleaf and peppercorns until well flavoured ; then strain off into a jug. Scrape (using a plastic scraper) or rinse out the pan, melt half the butter in the same pan and add the onion. Cook slowly until soft but without browning, then add the mushrooms and increase the heat. Cook briskly for 2-3 minutes, stirring occasionally. Then draw off the heat, add the rest of the butter and stir in the flour. Add the milk by degrees, blend thoroughly, and stir over heat until boiling. Draw aside again, to add the cream, yolk and seasoning. Turn on to a plate to cool.

Fill the flan with this mixture. Roll out the remaining pastry and cut into thin strips. Lay a diagonal lattice over the top of the flan, pressing the ends of the strips well down on to the edge. Cover edge with a strip of pastry to neaten. Beat the small egg with salt and brush over the flan. Bake for 25-35 minutes in pre-set oven.

Mushrooms Philippe

4-6 oz button mushrooms
1 large tablespoon olive oil
1 shallot (finely chopped)
1 wineglass red wine
1 teaspoon thyme (freshly chopped)
1-2 tablespoons French dressing (preferably made with red wine vinegar)
salt and pepper

Method

Wash and trim mushrooms (cut off stalks level with caps, slice stalks lengthways and put with mushroom caps).

Heat oil in a small frying pan, put in the mushrooms and the shallot. Fry briskly for about 3 minutes, turning and stirring them all the time.

Lift out mushroom mixture with a draining spoon into a bowl. Pour wine into the pan and boil until it is reduced by half. Add to the mushrooms with the herbs and French dressing. Season well, cover, and leave until cold.

Scalloped mushrooms

$\frac{1}{2}$-$\frac{3}{4}$ lb flat mushrooms
2 tablespoons fresh white breadcrumbs
$\frac{1}{2}$ oz butter (melted)
1 egg yolk
1-2 tablespoons cream, or top of milk
1 rounded teaspoon finely chopped parsley
1 rounded teaspoon chives
1 clove of garlic (crushed with salt)
salt and pepper
mornay sauce (made with $\frac{1}{2}$ oz butter, $\frac{1}{2}$ oz flour, $\frac{1}{2}$ pint milk, 1$\frac{1}{2}$ oz grated cheese, seasoning)
grated cheese (to sprinkle)
browned breadcrumbs
extra melted butter

4-6 scallop shells

Method

Set oven at 350°F or Mark 4.

Wash and peel mushrooms, remove stalks, and set aside 3-4 for each person. Chop stalks and peelings and any remaining mushrooms. Add fresh crumbs and bind with the butter, egg yolk and cream ; mix in the herbs, garlic and seasoning. Fill the whole mushrooms with this mixture and arrange them in buttered scallop shells, coat with mornay sauce. Sprinkle with cheese, browned crumbs and melted butter and bake in pre-set oven for 12-15 minutes.

Mushroom and game loaf

1 Coburg, or milk, loaf
1$\frac{1}{2}$ oz butter (melted)
1 egg (beaten)

For filling
8-12 oz cup, or flat, mushrooms
$\frac{3}{4}$ lb game (such as hare, rabbit, pigeon, etc., mixed or not)
butter (to sauté)
1 onion (finely chopped)
1 rounded tablespoon plain flour
7$\frac{1}{2}$ fl oz good stock (preferably game)
salt and pepper
pinch of mace
1 round tablespoon chopped mixed herbs and parsley

This is a good way of using the wings of hare or rabbit, which are not used in some recipes.

Method

Set oven at 350°F or Mark 4.

Cut cap off the loaf, scraping away any hard crust, and carefully scoop out the crumb. Brush inside and out with melted butter and then a beaten egg. Do the same to the 'lid'. Put both on a baking sheet and put in pre-set oven for 7-10 minutes until crisp and golden-brown.

Meanwhile prepare the filling : fry the onion in the rest of the melted butter, then add the flour with a little more butter if necessary to make a soft roux. Draw pan aside and blend in the stock. Season and bring to the boil. Simmer for 3-4 minutes, then add the herbs and draw pan aside.

Cut the game into shreds and add it to the sauce. Trim the mushrooms and sauté them quickly in a little extra butter. Put a layer of mushroom in the bottom of the loaf, turn the game mixture on top and cover with the rest of the mushrooms. Replace the lid, and put back in the oven for a further 7-10 minutes. Serve hot.

1 *Scooping out crumb from the loaf before brushing with melted butter and egg.*
2 *Filling baked crust with layers of mushrooms and game.*

1

2

Mushrooms in white wine

1 lb mushrooms
2 oz butter, or 3 tablespoons olive oil
2 large onions (finely sliced)
2 wineglasses white wine
bouquet garni
salt
pepper (ground from mill)
1 tablespoon chopped parsley

To serve
fingers of hot toast spread with anchovy butter, or crisp rolls and unsalted butter

To heat rolls : if you buy small white rolls from the baker, the best way to heat them without making them hard on the outside is to put the rolls in a paper bag and slip this into a hot oven for about 4-5 minutes. This way the rolls will get hot and crisp on the outside, without becoming hard.

Method

Trim the mushrooms, wash quickly in salted water and cut in thick slices. Heat the butter (or oil) in a sauté pan, add the mushrooms, sauté over quick heat for 1-2 minutes then remove from the pan. Reduce the heat, add the onions to pan and cook slowly until soft but not coloured ; tip on the white wine, add the bouquet garni and simmer until the wine is reduced by half. Return the mushrooms to the pan, season with salt and pepper from the mill and simmer for 5 minutes. Remove bouquet garni, tip the mushroom mixture into a hot gratin dish and dust with parsley.

Serve with fingers of hot toast spread with anchovy butter, or hot crisp rolls and unsalted butter.

1 *Slicing the onions and mushrooms after trimming and washing*
2 *Adding sauté mushrooms to pan of onions, wine and bouquet garni*

Mushroom cream

1 lb button mushrooms
$\frac{1}{4}$ pint chicken stock, or white wine
$\frac{1}{2}$ oz gelatine
1 cup celery (finely diced)
$\frac{1}{2}$ green pepper (diced and blanched)
salt and pepper
7 fl oz double cream
1 egg white

For garnish
4 oz prawns, or shrimps (shelled)
1 tablespoon tomato ketchup, or chutney
1 teaspoon red wine vinegar
dash of Tabasco sauce
1 dill cucumber
1 teaspoon chopped parsley

Ring mould (1 pint capacity)

Method

Lightly oil the ring mould. Slice the mushrooms, cook them very quickly in the stock or wine (2-3 minutes only). Drain off the liquid and measure out $7\frac{1}{2}$ fl oz. Take 5 tablespoons of this and dissolve the gelatine in it. Add the celery and green pepper to the mushrooms. Pour the dissolved gelatine into the rest of the liquid, stir it back into the pan containing the mushroom mixture and season well.

Whip the cream lightly and the egg white stiffly and combine the two. Fold into the mixture and, when setting, turn into the prepared ring mould. Leave in a cool place to set.

Mix the prawns (or shrimps), ketchup (or chutney), vinegar and Tabasco. Slice the dill cucumber and mix with parsley.

Turn the cream on to a serving dish, mix prawns and cucumber and spoon carefully into the centre of the mould.

Spiced jellied mushrooms

8 oz mushrooms
1 can turtle soup, or consommé
1 dessertspoon soy sauce
salt and pepper
2-3 drops of Tabasco sauce
dash of Worcestershire sauce
$\frac{1}{2}$ pint water
$\frac{1}{4}$ oz gelatine
lemon juice

To finish
lettuce
lemon quarters
brown bread and butter

Method

Trim mushrooms and wash them if necessary. Chop the trimmings and put into a pan with the soup or consommé, seasoning, sauces, water and mushrooms. Simmer mixture for 5-10 minutes, draw aside. Dissolve gelatine in a little of the liquid from the pan, add this to the mushrooms, adjust seasoning and sharpen with lemon juice. Turn into a flat dish or wet tin and leave to set.

To serve, cut salad across into squares and arrange on lettuce leaves. Serve with lemon quarters and brown bread and butter separately.

Fried onions

1 medium-size onion per person (finely sliced)
2-3 tablespoons dripping, or oil
granulated sugar (for dusting)

Method

Peel onion, slice a small piece off the side so that the onion remains firmly on the chopping board while slicing fairly finely across (not lengthways). Push slices out into rings.

To make onions more digestible, blanch after slicing by putting into cold water and bringing to the boil. Refresh by pouring cold water over and draining well on absorbent paper.

Put slices into the frying pan with hot fat or oil and fry fairly quickly, turning occasionally with a fork, dust with sugar to help them brown. When well browned take out and drain on absorbent paper before serving in heaps around, or on top of, steaks.

Glazed onions

Use button onions or shallots. Peel them and cover with cold water, add salt and bring to the boil. Tip off the water, add 1-1½ oz butter and a dusting of caster sugar. Cover and cook gently until golden-brown on all sides, and cooked through (about 10 minutes).

Onion ragoût (stew)

1 lb button onions, or shallots
1 oz butter
1 teaspoon granulated sugar
1 wineglass white wine, cider, or stock

Method

Peel onions, blanch in pan of cold water by bringing to boil. Drain and turn into a casserole, add butter, sugar and wine (or cider, or stock). Cover tightly, cook until tender (40-45 minutes) in oven pre-set at 350°F or Mark 4. Serve in the casserole.

Onion rings

Use large Spanish onions for crisp fried onion rings. Cut 1-2 large onions in ¼-inch slices and separate the rings. Barely cover them with milk, leave them to soak for 5 minutes, then drain. Dip rings in beaten egg, then in flour and fry in deep fat until crisp and golden-brown. Drain the rings on crumpled absorbent paper.

Casserole of onions and potatoes

$\frac{3}{4}$ lb button onions
1 oz butter
1 teaspoon granulated sugar
$\frac{1}{2}$ pint stock
1 lb new potatoes (scraped),
or 1 lb old potatoes (peeled and cut into small pieces),
or 1 can new potatoes
1 teaspoon chopped parsley (optional)

Method

Blanch onions by putting in pan of cold water and bringing to boil ; strain before further cooking. Return to a flameproof casserole with butter, sugar and stock. Boil gently until onions are tender and stock has reduced to about 2 tablespoons. Do not allow onions to brown.

Cook potatoes in boiling salted water, or heat canned ones. Drain and add to the onions with parsley. Serve in the casserole.

Onion tart

For rich shortcrust pastry
8 oz plain flour
pinch of salt and pepper
4 oz butter
2 oz lard
1 egg yolk
2-3 tablespoons cold water

For filling
4 large onions
3 oz butter
6-8 rashers of streaky bacon (diced)
3 large eggs
$\frac{1}{4}$ pint creamy milk
$2\frac{1}{2}$ fl oz cream, or evaporated milk
2-3 tablespoons Parmesan cheese
a little melted butter

9-inch diameter flan ring

Method

Prepare the pastry and chill it. Then roll out and line into the flan ring, making sure that the edge stands up $\frac{1}{4}$ inch above the ring. Prick the bottom with a fork and chill.

Meanwhile prepare the filling ; slice the onions finely, blanch, drain well and then return to the pan with the butter. Cook them until golden and quite tender, then tip into a bowl. Blanch the diced bacon and fry until crisp in the butter left in the pan from the onions. Add all to onions.

Beat the eggs with a fork, season, add milk and cream (or evaporated milk), then add to the onion mixture. Pour filling into the tart, sprinkle with Parmesan cheese and a little melted butter and bake in a hot oven, pre-set at 400°F or Mark 6, for 10-12 minutes to set the pastry ; then lower the heat to 375°F or Mark 5 and continue to cook for a further 20 minutes or until the egg mixture is golden-brown and set.

Watchpoint Set the flan ring on a pre-heated baking sheet to ensure that underneath of flan is cooked.

Onion and apple pie

6 oz quantity of rich shortcrust pastry
2 onions
1 lb good cooking apples
salt and pepper
1 teaspoon chopped sage
pinch of mixed spice
2 tablespoons clotted cream

7-inch diameter flan ring

This is a Cornish dish and can be eaten with meat or as a picnic snack. If clotted cream is not available, use 2 tablespoons double cream or 1 oz butter, thinly sliced.

Method

Set oven at 400°F or Mark 6. Slice the onions, then blanch and drain them. Peel, quarter and core apples. Roll out half the pastry and line the flan ring.

Slice the apples and put a layer on the pastry. Scatter over the onions, season well and add sage and spice. Slice in sufficient apple to fill the ring. Spread the cream on top. Roll out rest of the pastry and cover ring ; press round, trim and decorate. Bake in the pre-set oven for 35-40 minutes. Cool, then remove ring. Serve warm.

Buttered parsnips

1 lb parsnips
1 teaspoon salt
1-2 oz butter
black pepper (ground from mill)

Method

Peel and quarter the parsnips, put in a pan with cold water to cover and add salt. Put on the lid and boil gently for 40-45 minutes. Drain off the liquid, return the pan to a gentle heat and cook for 2-3 minutes to dry off any moisture.

It is wise to keep the lid on the pan at this stage as the parsnips stick to the pan and burn rather easily.

Crush parsnips with a fork or potato masher and add butter a small piece at a time. Season well and serve very hot.

Parsnip croquettes

2 large parsnips
a little beaten egg
3 tablespoons dried white breadcrumbs
2 oz butter (for frying)

Method

Cut the parsnips in fingerlength pieces (about 3 inches long by $\frac{3}{4}$ inch thick) and cook in salted water until tender (about 15 minutes) ; drain and return to pan, with $\frac{1}{2}$ oz of the butter, on a low heat to dry. Turn on to a plate to cool. Brush the parsnip pieces with the beaten egg and coat with the crumbs. Fry croquettes in hot butter until golden-brown.

Petits pois à la française

4 lb young green peas (2 pints shelled)
1 Cos lettuce (shredded)
12-14 small spring onions (cut in 2-inch lengths)
1 dessertspoon granulated sugar
bouquet garni
2 oz butter
¼ pint cold water
salt

Method

Put the peas in a pan with the shredded lettuce, spring onions, sugar, herbs and half the butter ; add the water. Instead of a lid, cover the pan with a deep plate filled with cold water and cook quickly for 25 minutes.

Note : the purpose of this plate containing cold water is to condense the steam as it rises from the peas while they cook. As the water in the plate evaporates, add more cold water.

Just 2 minutes before serving remove the bouquet garni, then add the remaining butter and salt to taste and shake the pan well to mix. Turn peas into a hot vegetable dish for serving.

Peas bonne femme

2-3 lb peas (1-1½ pints shelled)
4-6 rashers of green bacon
about 12 spring onions
1 oz butter
heart of 1 lettuce (shredded)
1 teacup light veal, or chicken, stock
salt and pepper
sprig of mint
kneaded butter (made with ½ oz butter, 1 dessertspoon flour)

The best type of peas to use for this dish are the small round ones, the French petits pois. This particular dish makes an excellent first course.

Method

Cut the bacon into lardons and blanch them. Trim the spring onions and cut in half, keeping a little of their green part on. Melt the butter in a pan, add the lardons and onions. Fry them gently until just coloured, then add the lettuce, peas and stock. Season, bring to the boil, add the mint, cover pan and simmer until peas are just tender (12-15 minutes).

Draw pan aside and add the kneaded butter, in small pieces. Shake the pan or stir gently until the kneaded butter has blended in, then reboil. Remove the sprig of mint and turn peas into a dish with a cover and serve.

Pease pudding

1 lb dried split peas (soaked overnight)
1 oz butter
1 egg
salt and pepper

This dish is traditionally served with boiled salt pork. Cooking is completed in the pan with the pork.

Method

Drain the peas, put them in enough cold salted water to cover well, and simmer until tender (about 1½ hours), adding more water if it reduces too much. Then drain and mash well or, if preferred, sieve or blend in an electric mixer.

Beat in the butter and egg and season well. Turn this mixture into a cloth or muslin, tie up and put into the pan with the pork for the last 35-45 minutes of cooking time. Turn pudding out of the cloth before serving.

Chick peas dish

8 oz dried chick peas (washed and soaked overnight in water)
1 medium-size onion (finely sliced)
2 oz butter
1 teaspoon cumin powder
½ teaspoon ground ginger
½ teaspoon chilli powder
1 teaspoon garam masala (see page 68)
1 small potato (boiled and diced)
1 tablespoon thick infusion of tamarind
salt
pinch of granulated sugar

Method

Simmer the peas in water until soft, drain them and keep the liquid. Fry the onions in the butter, add the spices and fry them gently for 1-2 minutes. Stir in 1 teacup of the reserved liquid and put in the peas and diced potato, bring to simmering point, add the infusion of tamarind, salt and sugar to taste. Cook gently for 10 minutes and serve with a meat curry.

Tamarind (imli) : the pod of the tamarind tree is used with a little sugar (gur) to give a sweet-acid effect. A piece about the size of an egg is added to ½ teacup of boiling water, left to infuse for 10 minutes, then squeezed through muslin. The resulting liquid is then used in a curry. For a thicker infusion use less water. If you cannot get any tamarind, substitute 1 tablespoon redcurrant jelly mixed with 1 tablespoon lemon or lime juice.

Sugar peas
(Mange-tout)

Apart from the usual varieties, there is a pea well known on the Continent as 'mange-tout' or, in England, the sugar pea. It is cultivated in the same way as the ordinary pea, and the pods, which are pale green and fleshy, are eaten whole with the very small peas left inside.

To prepare and cook : top and tail the pods and wash well. Then boil gently with just enough salted water to cover them. Allow 12-15 minutes cooking time. Drain thoroughly and return to the pan with a good knob of butter, salt and pepper. They can be served like this as an accompanying vegetable or, mixed with a little cream sauce or tomato sauce, served as a first course or entremets.

Sweet peppers

These may be green, red or yellow. The green are available throughout the year, the red and yellow between late July and the end of September. The flavour is mild. Canned red peppers are also available and are called pimentos or, more correctly, pimientos.

Fresh peppers are a good addition to fish and meat dishes as well as making an excellent dish on their own.

To prepare, split peppers in two and cut away the hard stalk. Scoop out and discard any seeds (these are hot). If to be shredded or cut in any way, blanch (put into boiling, salted water and when the water reboils, drain and refresh). The peppers are then ready for use according to the recipe and will be more digestible.

Stuffed peppers

5 red, or green, peppers
¾ pint tomato sauce

For stuffing
1 onion (finely chopped)
1½ oz butter
4 oz rice
2 oz mushrooms (chopped)
4 oz cooked ham, or veal, or chicken
salt and pepper
¾-1 pint veal, or chicken, stock

Method

Cut tops off peppers and scoop out seeds. Blanch for 2-3 minutes, pushing peppers down well under the water. Then drain, refresh and drain again. Pat them dry with a cloth and set aside. Set oven at 350°F or Mark 4.

To prepare stuffing : soften onion in 1 oz of the butter, add rice, stir over heat for 1-2 minutes, then add mushrooms and the meat. Season, pour over stock, bring to the boil, cover and put pan in the pre-set oven for 20 minutes, or until rice is tender and stock absorbed. Stir in the remaining butter with a fork.

Put this mixture in the peppers ; pack upright in a casserole. Heat the tomato sauce and pour over and round the peppers. Cover dish and continue cooking in oven for 25-30 minutes, or until peppers are tender.

Celery and green pepper chartreuse

packet of lime jelly
juice of ½ lemon
1 tablespoon onion juice
1 green pepper
1 cap of canned pimiento
¼ pint mayonnaise
4 sticks of celery (diced)
sprigs of watercress

Ring mould (2½ pints capacity)

Method

Break the jelly into cubes, pour on ½ pint boiling water, stir until dissolved, then add the lemon and onion juice, and make up to ¾ pint with cold water ; leave to cool.

Remove the core and seeds from the green pepper and cut the flesh in dice. Blanch these in boiling water for 1 minute, then drain and refresh. Dice the canned pimiento. When the jelly begins to thicken, whisk vigorously until it looks foamy, then fold in the mayonnaise and the prepared celery, pepper and pimiento. Pour into the mould, cover and leave to set.

When ready to serve, dip the mould quickly in and out of hot water, turn jelly on to a serving platter and garnish with sprigs of watercress.

Peperoni

2 green and 2 red peppers (halved, cored, seeds removed and thinly sliced)
1 oz butter
1 medium-size onion (sliced)
1 clove of garlic (crushed with ½ teaspoon salt)

Method
Prepare the peppers and blanch if wished. Melt the butter in a small pan, add the onion and crushed garlic and cook slowly until soft but not coloured, add the peppers and seasoning and cook until just tender.

Green pepper with tomato and avocado

1 green pepper (chopped and blanched)
6 even-size ripe tomatoes
1 avocado (diced)
1-2 spring onions (shredded)
2-3 tablespoons French dressing

Method
Scald and skin tomatoes, cut off tops and scoop out seeds.

Carefully mix prepared avocado, pepper and onion and moisten with French dressing. Fill the tomatoes, replace tops, arrange on a serving dish and spoon over a little French dressing with herbs added.

Sweet pepper relish

6 large green peppers
6 large red peppers
6 medium-size onions
1¼ pints white malt, or white wine, vinegar
1 rounded tablespoon salt
10 oz granulated sugar
1 rounded teaspoon mustard seed

Method
Split the peppers and remove the seeds. Chop flesh, or pass it through a mincer, and chop the onions. Put these into a bowl, pour on enough boiling water to cover and drain at once. Turn vegetables into a pan, cover with cold water, bring to the boil and drain again.

Put the vinegar, salt, sugar and mustard seed into the pan and bring to the boil. When the pepper mixture is well drained, stir it into the hot vinegar. Simmer for 20-25 minutes, until it is fairly thick, but not as thick as chutney. Turn into jars and cover with cellophane or a metal lid with a vinegar-proof coating (uncoated metal will corrode in contact with vinegar). Use this relish straight away for it does not keep as well as chutney.

Boiled potatoes

Home-grown new potatoes come into the shops in June, but it is often possible to buy imported ones from Christmas onwards. Old potatoes are best in autumn after the main crop is gathered.

To cook new potatoes : scrape and put into boiling salted water ; cover pan and boil for 20-30 minutes, or until tender. Drain, place over gentle heat for a few minutes to dry.

To cook old potatoes : peel thinly, put into cold salted water, bring to boil and cook covered for 20-30 minutes, or until tender. Drain and finish as above. If preferred, potatoes may be peeled after boiling.

Baked (jacket) potatoes

1 large potato per person
salt
pat of butter per person
parsley (optional)

Method

Well scrub large, even-size potatoes and roll them in salt. Bake for 1½ hours (or until they give when pressed) in an oven pre-set at 375°F or Mark 4. Make crosscuts on top of each potato and squeeze to enlarge cuts. Put a pat of butter and sprig of parsley in centre ; serve at once.

Creamed potatoes

1½ lb old potatoes
1-2 oz butter
¼ pint milk
salt and pepper

Method

Cut the peeled potatoes in even-size pieces if very large, and put into cold salted water. Bring to the boil and cook until tender (about 20 minutes). Test with the point of a fine knife or trussing needle ; do not test with the thick prongs of a fork or the potato will break.

Watchpoint Take care to cook potatoes in water and not let it boil away from them.

When potatoes are tender, tilt the lid of the pan and pour off all the water. Return to a gentle heat and, with the lid half-closed, continue cooking a few minutes until the potatoes are dry. Then add the butter — as much as you like — and crush the potatoes with a potato masher or a fork. Adjust seasoning. Press them down firmly to the bottom of the saucepan and pour over boiling milk (¼ pint is enough for 1½-2 lb potatoes). Do not stir, but put the lid on the saucepan, which should stand in a hot place until your main course is dished up. Creamed potatoes can be kept hot in this way for up to 30 minutes, and the potatoes will absorb the milk on standing. Just before dishing up, beat the potatoes very well with a wooden spoon, or small electric whisk, until fluffy.

Chip potatoes (French fried)

$1\frac{1}{2}$ lb even-size potatoes (weighed when peeled)
deep fat, or at least 1-inch depth of fat in frying pan

Method

Prepare potatoes 1 hour before needed. Square off ends and sides of potatoes, cut in $\frac{1}{2}$-inch thick slices, then into thick fingers. Soak in cold water for 30 minutes, then drain. Wrap in absorbent paper or cloth and leave for 20-30 minutes. Heat fat, dip in the empty basket; when fat reaches 350°F, gently lower potatoes in basket into fat. If you do not have a thermometer, drop in a finger of potato; if this rises to surface at once and fat starts to bubble gently, fat is ready. Fry gently until potatoes are just soft but not coloured. Lift out and drain, still in basket, on a plate. Chips can be left like this for a little while before the final frying. Reheat fat to 360-375°F; carefully lower in basket, fry chips to a deep golden-brown. Drain well on absorbent paper, turn into a hot dish for serving and sprinkle with salt. Potatoes double-fried in this way are crisply tender on the outside and evenly browned. When cooking fish and chips, fry potatoes first so that there is no chance of crumb coating from fish spoiling the fat for the potatoes.

Game chips

These chips are a traditional accompaniment to game.

Choose large potatoes ($1\frac{1}{2}$ lb will be sufficient for up to 6 people). Peel and trim off the ends and cut in very thin slices. Soak slices in a large bowl of cold water for 1 hour, separating slices to prevent them sticking together. Drain well and leave wrapped in a clean teacloth for 20 minutes, again separating the slices so that they dry thoroughly.

Fry the slices a few at a time in a basket in deep fat or oil heated to 350°F, and remove when bubbling subsides. When all slices have been cooked in this way, reheat the fat or oil to 375°F, put two or three batches of slices together in the basket and fry until they are golden-brown.

As soon as there is no danger of the fat bubbling over, turn potato slices out of basket into pan to finish cooking ; keep them separated with a draining spoon. Drain well on crumpled, absorbent paper and then pile on to a hot dish. Sprinkle with salt and serve.

Watchpoint Never cover up game chips or they will lose all their crispness.

Straw potatoes

Cut potatoes into sticks one-eighth of an inch thick, then into matchsticks, one-eighth of an inch wide. Soak in cold water for 30 minutes, then dry throughly. Fry as for game chips (above).

Baked (roast) potatoes

Choose medium to large potatoes of even size. Peel and blanch by putting into cold salted water and bringing to the boil. Drain thoroughly and lightly scratch the surface with a fork (this will prevent a dry and leathery exterior after cooking). Now put the potatoes into hot fat in the same tin as the meat, if you are cooking a joint, 40-45 minutes before the meat is fully cooked, and baste well. Cook until soft (test by piercing with a cooking fork or fine skewer), basting them when you baste the meat and turning after 25 minutes. Drain well on kitchen paper, pile in a vegetable dish and sprinkle with a little salt. Do not cover before serving.

Sauté potatoes

$1\frac{1}{2}$ lb potatoes
2 tablespoons oil
1 oz butter
salt and pepper
1 dessertspoon chopped parsley

Method

Scrub potatoes and boil in their skins until very tender. Then drain, peel and slice. After heating a frying pan put in oil, and when this is hot add the butter. Slip in all the potatoes at once, add seasoning and cook (sauté) until golden-brown and crisp, yet buttery, occasionally turning the contents of the pan. Draw aside, check seasoning, and add parsley. Serve in a very hot dish.

Maître d'hôtel potatoes

$1\frac{1}{2}$ lb even-size potatoes
$1\frac{1}{2}$ oz butter
1 shallot (chopped)
2 tablespoons chopped parsley
salt and pepper

Method
Scrub potatoes and boil or steam in their skins until tender but firm. Drain and dry. Peel potatoes, slice and arrange in a hot dish and keep warm.

Melt butter in a small pan, add shallot, cover pan and set on low heat for 2-3 minutes. Then draw aside, add parsley and plenty of seasoning and pour contents of pan over the potatoes. Slide into the oven for 2-3 minutes before serving.

Potato croquettes

1 lb potatoes
$\frac{1}{2}$ oz butter
1 egg yolk
2 tablespoons hot milk
salt and pepper
seasoned flour
1 egg (beaten)
dried white breadcrumbs
butter (for frying)

Method
Boil potatoes and press through a wire sieve, return to pan, beat in butter, egg yolk, hot milk and seasoning. Divide into cork-shaped pieces, roll in seasoned flour, brush with beaten egg, then roll in dried white breadcrumbs. Fry in butter until golden-brown.

Potato balls

$1\frac{1}{2}$ lb potatoes
1 oz butter
1 small onion (finely chopped)
1 egg yolk
salt and pepper
1 egg (beaten)
matzo meal (for coating)
deep oil (for frying)

Method
Peel potatoes and boil until tender, then sieve them.

Melt the butter and soften the onion in it over gentle heat in a covered pan. Add sieved potato, egg yolk and seasoning. Cool mixture slightly before rolling it in small balls. Coat balls with the beaten egg and roll in matzo meal. Fry in deep hot oil until golden and crisp, about 3-4 minutes. Then drain on absorbent paper and serve.

Julienne potato cake

1 lb potatoes (peeled)
1 oz butter
salt and pepper

Method

Although the potatoes may be peeled ahead of time, they must never be cut into strips until you are ready to cook them.

Cut the peeled potatoes into julienne strips. Dry well in a cloth or absorbent kitchen paper.

A heavy 6-inch diameter frying pan is ideal for these as a larger one makes it almost impossible to turn out the potato cake. Rub a thick, even coating of butter (1 oz) over the base and sides of the pan, press in the potatoes, season only when a thick layer covers the base, or the salt will make the potatoes stick. All the seasoning will be absorbed by the potatoes, none being thrown away as with the liquid from boiled potatoes.

If lid is not close-fitting, put a layer of overlapping, buttered paper between pan and lid to prevent loss of steam as this would result in potatoes over-browning or burning on the bottom before they are quite tender.

If cooked on top of stove, heat must be gentle and even (allow about 30-40 minutes). However, when entertaining, you may find it easier to combine top of stove and oven heat. In this case cook about 10-15 minutes on top of stove on a steady heat, testing colouring of strips by lifting lid, inserting a palette knife down side and taking a quick look. With experience your nose will tell you when potatoes are coloured by the unmistakable smell of beurre noisette (butter cooked to a nut-brown). At this stage transfer pan to oven below meat or chicken if oven is set at 400°F or Mark 6, or above if oven has been turned low. Since you have top heat only, there is no fear of the potatoes burning. Continue cooking for about 30 minutes. For final testing, use the point of a cooking knife.

If you want to make larger quantities than for 4-6 people, use 2 sandwich tins and lids made from foil with a plate on top. The pan or tin should be generously full, the weight of the plate (in the case of the tin) being used to press the potatoes down. In this case cook on top for 10 minutes only, finishing off in oven as above.

To serve, turn out the potato cake so that the browned part is facing up (see below). If serving with chicken, the chicken may be dished up on top of the potato cake with a little sauce or cooking juices spooned over it.

Anna potatoes

1½-2 lb potatoes
salt and pepper
2-3 oz butter

6-inch diameter thick frying pan with ovenproof handle, or cake tin

A **mandoline** is a rectangular piece of wood or metal fitted with a sharp blade, plain or fluted, which is used for slicing vegetables. The blade can be adjusted to regulate the thickness of the slice.

Method

Butter the frying pan or tin very generously. Slice the potatoes in thin rounds (a mandoline slicer is excellent for this) and arrange neatly in circles to cover the base of the pan. After two layers are in, season and add a few small pieces of butter. Continue to fill the pan, seasoning and buttering every other layer. Spread any remaining butter on a piece of foil and cover the pan securely.

Sit an ovenproof plate on top of the foil to give a little weight and prevent loss of steam during cooking. Set the pan on moderate heat for 15 minutes then put in the oven, pre-set at 350°F or Mark 4, for about 30 minutes to complete cooking. Turn out whole on to serving dish.
Note : if cooking potatoes with the meat in an oven set at 400°F or Mark 6, place potatoes on shelf below meat.

Using a mandoline to cut Anna potato slices

Arranging potato in circles in a frying pan

Julienne of potato and celery

3 even-size potatoes
1 head of celery
1 oz butter
1 shallot (finely chopped)
salt
black pepper (ground from mill)
chopped parsley — to garnish

Method

Peel potatoes, trim celery, and cut into julienne strips ($\frac{1}{8}$ inch thick by $1\frac{1}{2}$-2 inches long). Keep the potatoes in a bowl of cold water until wanted; this will help them keep their colour and also remove some of the starch present.

Heat the butter in a sauté pan or flameproof casserole, add the celery and shallot, cover and shake over the heat for 4-5 minutes. The vegetables should not colour and this part of the cooking can be done ahead.

Drain the potatoes and dry in a cloth; put them into the pan and season. Stir carefully to mix the celery and shallot into the potato, cover with greaseproof paper and a lid, and cook on top of the stove or in the oven, pre-set at 350°F or Mark 4, until the potatoes are tender (8-10 minutes). Dust with chopped parsley and dish up.

Note: if this dish is prepared and cooked straight through and a shallow pan is used on top of the stove, the potatoes will take about 8-10 minutes. However, if the cooking time is broken and the potatoes are put into a cold celery mixture and then in oven, allow 15-20 minutes.

Sicilian potatoes

½-¾ lb potatoes (3-4 medium-size ones)
1 small orange (preferably a blood orange)
pinch of bicarbonate of soda
4 oz butter
2 shallots (finely chopped)
salt and pepper
1 egg yolk (optional)

Method

First put the orange in a pan of water with a pinch of bicarbonate of soda and boil for 45-50 minutes. Peel the potatoes, then boil, drain and dry well and crush with a potato masher or push through a sieve. Turn them into a basin.

Set the oven at 400°F or Mark 6. Drain the orange, cut in four and remove any pips, then finely chop the quarters (including peel). Melt 2 oz of the butter in a small saucepan, add shallot and cook until coloured ; cook for 1-2 minutes more, then add chopped orange. Cook onion mixture, without the lid, until turning colour. Then mix with the sieved potato ; season well, add 1 oz butter, and the egg yolk if wished.

Melt the remainder of the butter, brush two baking sheets with it, then shape the mixture into large 'marbles'. Put these down the baking sheet at intervals and, with the prongs of a fork, flatten each marble to about ¼ inch thick. Bake in the pre-set oven for about 10-15 minutes or until well browned. Take the baking sheets out of the oven, slip a palette knife under each potato 'cake' and serve them overlapping on a hot dish, with the underside uppermost.

Boulangère potatoes

1½ lb old potatoes (thinly sliced)
3 medium-size onions
salt and pepper
¾ pint stock
1 bayleaf
1 tablespoon dripping

Method

Slice onions, blanch by putting in cold water, bring to the boil and boil for 1 minute before draining. Peel and slice potatoes in thin rounds and place immediately in a fireproof dish layered with the onions, salt and pepper. Pour over just enough stock to cover and add bayleaf. Dot well with dripping and bake for 1 hour in oven, pre-set at 400°F or Mark 6, until tender and well browned.

To get the best results, remove from oven halfway through cooking time when, if top layer of potatoes has curled up, press down into the stock with basting spoon and add a little extra dripping, if necessary.

Parisienne potatoes

Scoop out potato balls with a cutter, either plain boil them and toss in melted butter, or sauté them ; add chopped parsley.

Potato goulash

$1\frac{1}{2}$ lb small new potatoes
1 tablespoon oil, or lard
$\frac{1}{2}$ lb onions (finely chopped)
$\frac{1}{2}$ clove of garlic (finely chopped)
1 dessertspoon paprika pepper
1 dessertspoon plain flour
2 tablespoons wine vinegar
$\frac{1}{4}$-$\frac{1}{2}$ pint stock, or water
salt and pepper
$\frac{1}{2}$ teaspoon caraway seeds (optional)
1 green pepper (sliced and blanched)
2 tomatoes (skinned, seeds removed, shredded)
2 tablespoons yoghourt, or soured, or fresh, cream

Method

Cook the potatoes in boiling salted water for 15 minutes. Meanwhile heat the oil (or lard) in a flameproof casserole, add the onions and garlic and cook slowly until golden-brown, stir in the paprika pepper and continue cooking for 1 minute. Remove from heat, blend in flour, vinegar and stock (or water). Season, bring to boil.

Drain the potatoes and put in the casserole with the caraway seeds (if used), green pepper and tomatoes ; cook for 5-10 minutes until potatoes are tender.

Just before serving, spoon the yoghourt or cream over the potatoes ; shake pan gently to blend cream with the sauce.

Lyonnaise potatoes

Slice and fry one onion until brown, then remove from pan and sauté the potatoes (see page 94). When these are brown, add the cooked onion slices.

Fondant potatoes

2-$2\frac{1}{2}$ lb small new potatoes
1 -2 oz butter
salt

Method

Scrape the potatoes, rinse well in cold water and dry in a tea towel. Melt the butter in a sauté pan, add the potatoes, cover and set over a very moderate heat. Shake the pan from time to time to turn the potatoes, but do not lift the lid for the first 10-15 minutes as the steam not only helps the potatoes to cook more quickly, but also prevents sticking. Test to see if the potatoes are tender, season with salt and turn on to a hot serving dish.

Potatoes aurore

1-1½ lb small new potatoes
sprig of mint
¼ oz butter

For sauce aurore
½ lb fresh tomatoes, or 1 cup canned tomatoes
1 clove of garlic (crushed)
¼ bayleaf
½ oz butter
1-2 tablespoons cream

For béchamel sauce
1½ oz butter
1¼ oz plain flour
¾ pint flavoured milk
salt and pepper

Method

Scrape potatoes, put them into pan of boiling salted water with mint and simmer for 5-6 minutes.

Meanwhile, cook tomatoes with the garlic, bayleaf and butter until reduced to a thick pulp. When reduced, put tomato pulp through a strainer (this should yield about 4-5 fl oz).

Prepare the béchamel sauce, beat in strained tomato pulp, season to taste and finish with the cream. Drain the potatoes, add ¼ oz butter and pour the sauce over them ; shake the pan gently and continue to cook potatoes for 5-6 minutes, or until tender.

Potato dumplings

1½ lb potatoes
1 slice of bread (crust removed)
½-1 oz butter
good pinch of ground mace
1 small egg
2 oz plain flour
½ oz cornflour
salt and pepper
melted butter (for serving)

Method

Scrub potatoes and boil in their skins until really tender. Drain and peel them, then put through a sieve or mash well. Leave until cold.

Meanwhile cut the bread into large dice and fry in the butter until brown. Now add the mace, egg and 2 kinds of flour to the potato and season. Mix well and shape into balls the size of a golf ball. Press 2 pieces of the fried bread into the middle of each dumpling, making sure that the potato covers the bread well.

Have ready a large pan full of boiling salted water and slip the dumplings into the water, being sure not to fill the pan too full — there should only be one layer. Boil gently with the lid off the pan for 12-15 minutes, turning the dumplings occasionally, then drain them well and serve hot with a little melted butter poured over the top.

Potatoes duxelles

1-1½ lb small new potatoes

For sauce
1½ oz butter
1 dessertspoon finely chopped onion
¼ lb dark, flat mushrooms (chopped)
1 rounded tablespoon plain flour
¾ pint strong chicken, or veal, stock
½ bayleaf
1 dessertspoon chopped mint

Method

First prepare the sauce: melt the butter, add the onion and, after 2-3 minutes, the chopped mushrooms, including the stalks; cook sauce for 3-4 minutes, then stir in the flour and stock and stir until sauce boils. Add the bayleaf and cook sauce gently for 6-8 minutes.

Meanwhile peel and boil the potatoes, drain them and add to the sauce; heat thoroughly and add the mint. Serve potatoes hot as an accompaniment.

Potatoes duxelles, served hot, have a mushroom and onion sauce and are garnished with chopped mint

Potatoes in white sauce (with parsley)

1 large can new potatoes (about 1 lb 3 oz)
chopped parsley

For white sauce
1½ oz butter
1¼ oz plain flour
¾ pint milk
salt and pepper

Canned new potatoes will save time and labour in the kitchen. They are delicious with hot ham served in a white sauce with chopped parsley.

Method

Prepare white sauce by first making a roux, blending in the milk and seasoning. Drain the potatoes, add them to the sauce and heat carefully without boiling ; then add the parsley and serve.

Note : to save time we would put the previously made white sauce into a double saucepan for reheating and then add potatoes when the sauce is hot. In this way there would be no danger of the potatoes boiling. (We mention this point as instructions on cans of new potatoes always say reheat without boiling.) Add the chopped parsley just before turning the potatoes into the serving dish.

Potatoes indienne

1-1½ lb small new potatoes
1½ oz butter
1 shallot (finely chopped)
1 dessertspoon curry powder
1 oz plain flour
1 pint milk
salt and pepper
1 bayleaf

Method

Wash potatoes, plunge them into boiling water, cook them gently for 5 minutes, then drain and peel them.

Melt the butter in a pan, add the shallot and curry powder. Cook them gently for 1-2 minutes, then stir in the flour, add the milk, stir until it is boiling, season and cook gently for 3-4 minutes to reduce it slightly in quantity.

Add the bayleaf and the potatoes to sauce, shake the pan rather than stir to make sure that the potatoes are under the surface of the sauce. Cover the pan and continue to cook for about 7-8 minutes until potatoes are tender (this depends on the size of the potatoes). If it is more convenient, the potatoes and sauce may be put into a covered casserole and cooked in the oven at 350°F or Mark 4 for 7-8 minutes.

Potatoes with white wine

1-1½ lb small new potatoes
1 wineglass white wine
1½ oz butter
salt and pepper
1 rounded tablespoon chopped mixed herbs (parsley, mint, and a little thyme)

This recipe can also be used for small new carrots.

Method

Scrape the potatoes and boil until tender or, if preferred, boil them in their skins, then peel. Return potatoes to the rinsed-out pan, pour over the white wine while they are still hot ; set pan over quick heat until liquid is reduced to about half.

Watchpoint Be sure to get the white wine well reduced, ie., almost to a syrup, before adding the butter.

Then add the butter in 2-3 pieces, shake pan well until it is melted, add seasoning and herbs. Turn potatoes into a dish and serve hot.

Potato gnocchi

1 lb potatoes (weighed when peeled)
nut of butter (about ½ oz)
4 tablespoons plain flour
salt and pepper
1 egg (beaten)
melted butter (for serving)

Method

Boil the potatoes, drain and dry them well. Put them through a ricer or wire sieve on to a board or table, or crush them with a potato masher. Cool potato a little before working in the butter, flour, seasoning and egg (add only enough egg to bind, avoiding any stickiness).

When well mixed and smooth, roll out mixture under the palms of both hands to a sausage shape, then cut off into small pieces. Roll each piece under the flat part of a fork. Turn these into a pan of gently simmering salted water and poach for 10-12 minutes, or until firm. Drain them well, turn into a hot dish and spoon over a little melted butter.

Maryland potatoes

$1\frac{1}{2}$ lb potatoes (peeled)
$\frac{1}{2}$ oz butter
1 can (7 oz) sweetcorn kernels
salt and pepper
$\frac{1}{2}$-$\frac{3}{4}$ pint hot milk
5-6 rashers of streaky bacon (thinly cut)

This is a good accompaniment to roast chicken.

Method

Cut potatoes into $\frac{1}{2}$-inch cubes, place in a buttered ovenproof casserole with the sweetcorn and a little seasoning. Pour over just enough hot milk to cover.

Put potatoes in oven, pre-set at 400°F or Mark 6, and leave for about $\frac{1}{2}$ hour. Then remove potatoes from oven, place rashers of bacon over the top and return to the oven. Continue baking until the bacon is brown and crisp. Allow 10-15 minutes for this. If bacon is still not as crisp as you like, slide the whole dish under the grill.

Latkes (potato cakes)

2 lb potatoes
2 oz self-raising flour
salt and pepper
1 egg (beaten)
oil (for frying)
3 tablespoons caster sugar
1 teaspoon cinnamon

Method

Peel the potatoes and grate, or mince finely, into cold water. Strain them well, squeezing in muslin to remove the water. Place the potato in a bowl, add flour, seasoning and beaten egg ; mix well.

Heat the oil in a frying pan, gently drop tablespoons of the mixture into the pan and fry until golden-brown, turning the cakes once. Drain them well. Dust with the mixed sugar and cinnamon and serve hot.

These cakes can be served either as a dessert or, without the sugar and cinnamon, as an accompanying vegetable dish.

Potato scones

1½ lb floury, freshly boiled potatoes
salt
6 oz plain flour

Girdle

This recipe makes approximately 12 scones.

These scones, which are different in shape and texture to drop scones, are equally good eaten cold or fried with the breakfast bacon. Made in large farls (large rounds marked in four), they are thin and flexible.

Method

Crush or sieve potatoes on to a floured board. Add salt to taste, work in the flour gradually, kneading it lightly and carefully.

Roll out mixture as thinly as possible. Cut into rounds the size of a dinner plate, then cut each round into quarters. Bake scones on a moderately hot girdle for 7-10 minutes, turning them once only.

Potato omelet

1-2 medium-size potatoes (diced)
¼ oz butter
few leaves of rosemary (optional)
4 - egg omelet

Method

This can be made with cooked or raw potato. Dice finely and brown in butter ; add rosemary while frying. Make a plain omelet and spoon in potato before folding over.

Salsify

There are two types of salsify. The white one is a winter parsnip — like vegetable and is better known than the black-skinned one, generally called scorzonera. Of the two, the latter is considered the finer.

To prepare and cook : scrape or peel white salsify ; scrub the scorzonera. Boil in salted water for 30-35 minutes, or until tender. Drain, peel scorzonera, and return to the pan with about 1 oz butter and seasoning, or serve au gratin, or in a good cream sauce.

Scorzonera with scrambled eggs

2-3 roots scorzonera
4-5 eggs
1½ oz butter
squeeze of lemon juice
2 tablespoons creamy milk
salt and pepper
croûtons of fried bread

Method

Wash and boil the scorzonera as above. Peel and cut into dice. Melt half the butter in a pan, add the scorzonera and sauté over moderate heat for 4-5 minutes, adding the lemon juice. Beat the eggs with a fork, add the milk and seasoning. Add remaining butter to pan, pour in the eggs and scramble gently. When just set, pour on to a hot dish and serve with croûtons.

Casserole of salsify

1½ lb salsify (scorzonera, or white)
1 oz butter
1 medium-size onion (chopped)
2 oz mushrooms (sliced)
1 dessertspoon plain flour
1 wineglass white wine
½ pint stock
salt and pepper
½ lb tomatoes, or 1 cup canned tomatoes
1 tablespoon freshly chopped herbs, or parsley
Parmesan cheese (grated) — for serving

Method

If necessary cut salsify into 3-4 inch lengths; boil the salsify until tender, then drain.

Melt the butter in a flameproof casserole, add onion and, after a few minutes, the mushrooms. Cook for 3 minutes, then stir in flour; add wine and stock. Season, bring to the boil and simmer for 7-8 minutes.

Then add salsify, the tomatoes (skinned, seeds removed, and chopped) and herbs. Simmer for 5 minutes, then serve with a separate dish of grated Parmesan cheese.

Seakale

This is one of the best and most prized of vegetables to serve as a special course. Unfortunately it seldom appears in the shops and then only in the winter months, usually around Christmas time. It is quite expensive to cultivate, as well as to buy, but for the enthusiast it is worth the trouble and cost.

Seakale does grow wild round our coasts but for the table it is forced and blanched. The stems are of pencil thickness but widening towards the root and are white with a grey-green tip.

Trim away the root and tie into bundles for cooking. Boil gently in salted water for about 16-20 minutes or until just tender. Drain thoroughly and serve on a folded napkin.

Serve hollandaise sauce (see page 14) or melted butter separately.

Boiled spinach

2-3 lb spinach
$\frac{3}{4}$ oz butter

Method

Wash the spinach thoroughly, remove stalks and any thick centre ribs. Cook in plenty of boiling salted water for 5-8 minutes, then drain well in a colander. Press between two plates to get rid of as much water as possible.

Melt butter in a saucepan, allow to colour slightly, then add the spinach and toss until dry. Serve.

Spinach cream with mornay sauce

2 lb spinach
$1\frac{1}{2}$ oz butter
4 rounded tablespoons fresh white breadcrumbs
$\frac{1}{2}$ cup of hot milk
1 egg
1 egg yolk
salt and pepper
browned breadcrumbs (for dusting)
grilled bacon rashers (to garnish)
sauté mushrooms (to garnish)
mornay sauce

6-inch diameter mould, or cake tin

Method

Wash spinach thoroughly, cook for 7 minutes in plenty of boiling water. Drain and press to remove excess water. Put through a Mouli sieve or work in a blender. Turn into a pan with butter and cook for 3-4 minutes to drive off some of the moisture. When it is a fairly firm purée, draw aside and cool.

Soak fresh white crumbs in hot milk and add to the spinach with beaten egg and extra yolk. Season well and turn into a buttered mould or cake tin dusted out with the browned crumbs. Fill completely, cover with buttered paper. Stand mould or tin in a roasting tin, pour boiling water round and cook in the oven, pre-set at 350°F or Mark 4, for about 45 minutes or until firm to the touch.

Remove mould or tin from hot water and leave for 2-3 minutes before turning out into a serving dish. Surround with grilled bacon and sauté mushrooms. Serve the mornay sauce separately.

Spinach creams

2 lb spinach
½ oz butter
béchamel sauce (made with 1 oz butter, 1 oz flour and ½ pint flavoured milk)
2 eggs
salt and pepper
grate of nutmeg

8 dariole moulds

Method

Cook the spinach in a large pan of boiling salted water for 7 minutes ; drain, refresh and press between two plates to remove the excess water. In this way the delicate leaves remain whole and unbroken. Carefully lift 8 spinach leaves (16 if they are small) and use to line the buttered moulds ; sieve the remaining leaves.

Melt the butter, cook slowly to a nutbrown, add the spinach purée and stir over the heat until dry. Add the béchamel sauce and mix well. Draw aside. Beat in the eggs, season well with salt and pepper and a tiny grate of nutmeg.

Spoon mixture into prepared moulds, cover with buttered paper or foil and cook au bain-marie in the oven, pre-set at 350°F or Mark 4 for 15-20 minutes.

Spinach creams are served here with braised lambs tongues coated in sauce

Spinach galette

1½-2 lb spinach
1-1½ oz butter
salt and pepper
4 large, or 5 small, eggs
¼ teacup creamy milk
little grated cheese (to finish)

For tomato coulis
¾ lb tomatoes (scalded, skinned, seeds removed, sliced)
½ oz butter
1 bunch of spring onions (trimmed)
1 dessertspoon plain flour
¼ teacup stock (optional)

This quantity of spinach should make four galettes each of about 5-6 inches in diameter. Serve as a first course.

Method

Boil the spinach for 5-8 minutes, press it dry, then sieve or pass it through a blender. Turn it into a bowl, add about ½ oz butter, season and mix together. Beat in the eggs, one at a time, add the milk and set bowl aside.

Watchpoint The amount of spinach when cooked should be 1 rounded tablespoon per egg ; the consistency of the mixture, once the eggs and milk have been added, should be that of thick cream.

To prepare tomato coulis : melt butter in a pan, add spring onions, with some of the green left on, cover pan and cook until they are just tender. Draw pan aside, sprinkle in the flour, add tomatoes and season. Cover pan and cook them to a pulp, adding stock if necessary.

To cook galettes : heat a small omelet or frying pan, put in remaining butter, pour in enough spinach mixture to cover the bottom by about a good ¼ inch. Cook this fairly slowly and, when set, slip a slicer underneath and turn galette over. Cook it a few seconds on this side, then slip it on to a hot serving dish. Spread with a good tablespoon of coulis and keep warm. Cook the remaining galettes, sandwiching coulis between each one, and pour the remaining coulis around them.

Grate a little cheese over the top, cut galettes like a cake and serve at once.

Spinach pancakes

½ pint pancake batter

For filling
1 lb spinach
1½ oz butter (plus a little melted)
1 shallot (finely chopped)
2 teaspoons tomato purée
4 tomatoes (peeled and roughly chopped)
1 teaspoon paprika pepper
4 eggs (hard-boiled and sliced)
salt
black pepper (ground from mill)
1 tablespoon Parmesan cheese (grated)

Method

Prepare pancake batter, leave in a cool place for 30 minutes.

Cook spinach in plenty of boiling water, drain thoroughly and set aside. Melt 1 oz butter, add shallot and cook slowly until soft but not coloured. Stir in tomato purée, tomatoes and paprika pepper and simmer for 2-3 minutes. Add slices of hard-boiled eggs and season.

Fry thin pancakes and spread with spinach, heated through in butter. Put 1 tablespoon of egg mixture on each one and roll up.

Place in a hot ovenproof dish, sprinkle with a little melted butter and grated cheese and brown lightly under the grill.

Gratin florentine

1 lb frozen leaf spinach
¼ pint milk
4 eggs (beaten)
4 egg yolks (beaten)
salt
pepper (ground from mill)
¼ pint single cream
little nutmeg (freshly grated)
8 oz long grain rice (cooked)
4 oz Cheddar cheese (grated)
1 oz Parmesan cheese (grated)

Method

Allow the spinach to thaw, press between 2 plates to remove the excess moisture, then chop finely. Set the oven at 375°F or Mark 5.

Heat the milk, tip it on to the beaten eggs and yolks, season well and add the cream and nutmeg.

Butter an ovenproof dish and fill with layers of spinach, rice and Cheddar cheese, beginning and ending with spinach ; pour over the egg mixture. Mix any remaining Cheddar cheese with the Parmesan and sprinkle this over the top. Cook au bain-marie in the pre-set oven till brown and crisp on the top, about 30 minutes.

Omelet Germiny

6 eggs
1 large handful of sorrel
2 large handfuls of spinach
$2\frac{1}{2}$-3 oz butter
salt and pepper
1 small carton ($2\frac{1}{2}$ fl oz) double cream
$\frac{1}{2}$ pint mornay sauce
$\frac{1}{2}$ lb spring onions
Gruyère cheese (grated)

Method

Blanch the sorrel and spinach together, then drain, press and chop. Put this into a pan with 1 oz of the butter, season, cover and cook for 4-5 minutes. Take off the lid and increase the heat to drive off any moisture ; add the cream and simmer uncovered for 2-3 minutes, then draw aside.

Note : if sorrel is not available (it can only be grown in a garden or gathered wild in the spring) use a good-size lettuce. Do not blanch this, but shred and cook straight away in butter with the spinach.

Prepare mornay sauce. Trim the onions, leaving on 1-2 inches of green, and blanch for 5-6 minutes, then drain and return to the pan with $\frac{1}{2}$ oz of the butter. Simmer for 2-3 minutes, then set aside.

Break the eggs into a bowl, beat to a froth, season and add 2 tablespoons water. Make the omelet, using the rest of the butter, and when creamily set spread the spinach mixture on top. Roll up and tip on to an ovenproof serving dish. Coat with the mornay sauce, sprinkle with the grated cheese and glaze under the grill. Garnish with the spring onions and serve the omelet at once.

Spinach roulade

1 lb spinach
$\frac{1}{2}$ oz butter
salt and pepper
4 eggs (separated)
Parmesan cheese (grated)

For filling
6 oz mushrooms (thinly sliced)
$\frac{1}{2}$ oz butter
1 rounded dessertspoon plain flour
salt and pepper
$\frac{1}{4}$ pint milk
little grated nutmeg
2-3 tablespoons cream (optional)

Swiss roll tin, or paper case (12 inches by 8 inches)

Method

Cook spinach in boiling salted water for about 8 minutes, drain well, press and pass through a sieve. Stir in butter, seasoning and egg yolks, one at a time. Whip the whites to a firm snow and fold into the mixture, using a metal spoon.

Set oven at 400°F or Mark 6. Have tin ready, lined with buttered greaseproof paper. Turn the mixture on to this, spread out quickly to about $\frac{1}{2}$ inch thick and dust well with cheese. Bake in pre-set oven on top shelf for about 10 minutes until well risen and firm to the touch.

Sauté mushrooms in butter, remove from heat and add the flour with seasoning to taste. Pour on the milk and bring to the boil, simmer to a creamy consistency, draw pan off heat. Stir in grated nutmeg and the cream.

Remove cooked roulade from oven, turn out on to a sheet of greaseproof paper, quickly peel off the paper on which it was cooked, spread with the mushroom filling and roll up.

Spinach soufflé

$1\frac{1}{2}$ lb spinach, or 1 large packet of frozen spinach purée
$\frac{1}{2}$ oz butter
salt and pepper
pinch of ground mace, or grated nutmeg
3 egg yolks
4 egg whites
1 tablespoon grated cheese
1 tablespoon browned breadcrumbs

For sauce
1 oz butter
1 rounded tablespoon plain flour
salt and pepper
$\frac{1}{4}$ pint milk

7-inch diameter top (size No. 1) soufflé dish

Method

Tie a band of greaseproof paper round soufflé dish so that it extends above rim of dish by 3 inches, butter inside of dish and paper rim. Set oven at 375°F or Mark 5.

Trim and wash spinach, boil in salted water for 8 minutes, drain and press well. Pass through a sieve, turn back into pan and stir over moderate heat to drive off excess moisture. Add the butter, season and set pan of spinach aside.

If using frozen spinach, put into a large pan on a gentle heat until completely thawed. Then increase heat to drive off excess moisture, add butter, seasoning and set aside.

To prepare sauce : melt the butter, remove pan from heat, stir in flour, then season and blend in milk. Add this to the spinach with the mace or nutmeg and additional seasoning to taste.

Beat in the egg yolks one at a time. Whip the whites to a firm snow, then cut and stir 1 tablespoon into the mixture, using a metal spoon. Stir in remainder of whites and turn into the prepared dish. Sprinkle top with cheese and browned crumbs mixed together. Bake for 25-30 minutes in pre-set oven until well risen and firm to the touch.

Spinach tart

For rich shortcrust pastry
6 oz plain flour
3 oz butter
1 oz shortening
1 egg yolk
1-2 tablespoons water (to mix)

For filling
1 lb spinach
1 oz butter
1 small onion (finelly sliced)
1 egg
1 large egg yolk
½ pint single cream
salt and pepper
1 tablespoon grated Parmesan cheese

7-inch diameter flan ring

Method

Prepare the shortcrust pastry and line into the flan ring; prick the bottom well with a fork.

To prepare the filling, cook spinach, drain and refresh and press between two plates to extract all the water. Chop spinach roughly. Melt the butter in a saucepan, add the onion, cook for 2-3 minutes until soft but not coloured, then add spinach and cook over a brisk heat to drive off any moisture. Tip into a bowl and allow to cool.

Set the oven at 375°F or Mark 5. Beat the egg and egg yolk with a fork, add the cream and season. Mix into the spinach mixture. Pour into the prepared flan case, dust the top with Parmesan cheese and bake in the pre-set oven for 30 minutes.

Watchpoint It is important to get the underneath of the pastry well cooked without overcooking the custard mixture. Put a second baking sheet into the oven while it is heating. The flan, on its baking sheet, is then placed on top of the hot baking sheet for cooking.

Creamed swedes

1 lb swedes
1 oz butter
black pepper
1 small carton ($2\frac{1}{2}$ fl oz) double cream

Method

Peel swedes, cut into even size wedges and cook in salted water until tender. Drain well and return to the heat to dry. Crush with a potato masher or fork, add the butter and continue cooking over gentle heat until all the water has gone. Season and pour in the cream just before serving the swedes.

Swede soufflé

4 tablespoons creamed swede (well seasoned)
2 oz butter
1 oz plain flour
$\frac{1}{4}$ pint milk
salt and pepper
3 egg yolks
4 egg whites
1 tablespoon browned crumbs

7-inch diameter top (size No. 1) soufflé dish

Method

Tie a band of greaseproof paper round the outside of the soufflé dish so that it extends above the rim of the dish by 3 inches. Butter inside of dish and paper and dust dish with browned crumbs. Set oven at 375°F or Mark 5.

Prepare the creamed swede as left. Melt the butter, stir in the flour off the heat and blend in the milk. Add the swede purée and bring slowly to the boil. Season well and beat in the egg yolks one at a time.

Whip the egg whites to a firm snow, then cut and stir 1 tablespoon into the mixture using a metal spoon. Stir in the remainder of the whites and turn into the prepared dish.

Dust with browned crumbs and bake in the pre-set oven until well risen and firm to the touch (about 25-30 minutes).

Tomatoes bruxelloise

8 even-size tomatoes
salt and pepper
1 small clove of garlic
$\frac{1}{2}$ pint mayonnaise
8 oz frozen prawns, or shrimps (chopped)
2 tablespoons double cream
1 bunch of watercress (to garnish)

Method

Scald and skin the tomatoes, slice off the tops, scoop out and discard the seeds ; season the insides and set aside.

Crush the garlic with a little salt and add it to the mayonnaise with the chopped prawns and cream. Fill tomatoes with the mixture, replacing the tops. Dish up and decorate with the bunch of watercress.

Tomato and sausage casserole

1 large can ($1\frac{3}{4}$ lb) tomatoes
$1\frac{1}{2}$ lb pork sausages
2 tablespoons good dripping
2 large onions (chopped)
1 oz plain flour
2 green peppers (seeded and chopped)
salt and pepper
granulated sugar (to taste)
1 tablespoon Worcestershire sauce
1 bayleaf
2 tablespoons browned breadcrumbs and 1 tablespoon grated Parmesan cheese (mixed) — optional

Method

Melt the dripping in a pan, add the onion and cook slowly until golden. Blend in the flour, add the tomatoes and peppers and stir until boiling. Season, add sugar, Worcestershire sauce and the bayleaf. Simmer for 30–40 minutes.

Meanwhile parboil the sausages for 10 minutes and remove their skins. Cut into thick, slanting slices.

Remove the bayleaf from the sauce. Add the sausages and tip the mixture into a pie dish. Sprinkle the top with the browned breadcrumbs and grated cheese ; bake in the oven, pre-set at 375°F or Mark 5, for 30 minutes.

Serve with French bread.

Tomato coulis

1 lb tomatoes (skinned, seeds removed and sliced)
1 Spanish onion (sliced in rings)
1 tablespoon oil, or dripping

Serve with braised beef.

Method

Fry onion rings until just brown in the dripping in a frying pan. Then add the prepared tomatoes. Season, cover pan and cook for 2-3 minutes only until tomatoes are just soft.

Spicy tomato coulis

1 medium-size can tomatoes
1 clove of garlic (crushed with ½ teaspoon salt)
1 teaspoon sugar
¼ pint stock, or cooking liquid from meat

Method

Put all the ingredients into a pan and simmer until the mixture is thick and pulpy. Serve with stuffed breast of mutton.

Tomatoes au fromage

1 lb ripe tomatoes (skinned)
salt and pepper
3 shallots
3 oz cheese (grated Parmesan and Gruyère mixed)
2-3 tablespoons browned breadcrumbs
1½ oz butter

Method

Set the oven at 375°F or Mark 5. Halve the tomatoes, flick out seeds, season the halves and arrange in an ovenproof dish. Chop the shallots very finely and scatter them over the tomatoes. Add the cheese to the crumbs and cover each tomato half with this mixture. Melt the butter, spoon it carefully over the tomatoes and bake in the pre-set oven for about 10 minutes, until the tomatoes are tender.

Stuffed tomatoes

4 large even-size tomatoes
4 tablespoons minced cooked cold beef, or lamb, or pork
1½ oz butter
2 small pickling onions (finely chopped)
2 tablespoons fresh white breadcrumbs
salt and pepper
1 tablespoon tomato ketchup
pinch of mixed herbs
1 tablespoon gravy
2 slices of bread (for toast)

Method

Set the oven at 375°F or Mark 5. Cut a slice from the top (not stalk end) of each tomato ; this means the tomato will sit well on the toast when served and the lid will look neater.

Rest the tomatoes very carefully in the hollow of your hand and scoop out the seeds and core with the point of a teaspoon. Strain the juice from the seeds and set aside. Put the meat in a basin.

Melt 1 oz butter in a small pan, put in the onions, cover and cook slowly until golden-brown. Add the onions and breadcrumbs to the meat, season well with salt and pepper. Mix in the ketchup with the juice from the tomato seeds and work into the meat and crumb mixture with a fork. Add the herbs and gravy.

Fill the tomatoes with mixture and put back the lid on the slant. Toast the bread, remove the crusts and cut out a square for each tomato. Butter the toast, set a tomato on each, cover with buttered paper and bake for 15-20 minutes in pre-set oven.

Filling tomatoes with stuffing mixture before placing on toast

Cooked stuffed tomatoes ready to be served on squares of toast

Tomatoes frankfurter

6 medium to large tomatoes
2 frankfurters
6 oz lean sliced ham (shredded)
2 oz Belgian liver sausage
French dressing
chopped herbs
salt and pepper

Method

Scald and skin tomatoes, cut off tops and scoop out seeds. Blanch the frankfurters for 5 minutes, cool and slice ; mix with the shredded ham and the liver sausage cut in large dice. Moisten with the dressing, add herbs and season. Fill tomatoes, replace 'lid' and chill.

Tomato sambal

3 tomatoes (skinned and chopped)
1 medium sized onion (finely chopped)
2-3 coriander leaves (chopped)
1 tablespoon lemon juice
pinch of caster sugar
salt

Method

Mix all ingredients together, adding the salt to taste. Serve with curries.

Tomatoes stuffed with Roquefort cream

8 even-size tomatoes
salt and pepper
2 eggs (hard-boiled)
3 sticks of tender celery (taken from centre of the head) — finely diced
3 oz Roquefort cheese
2 tablespoons double cream
4 tablespoons French dressing
1 teaspoon chopped chives

Method

Scald and skin tomatoes. Cut off the tops from the smooth end and carefully scoop out the seeds and core, using a teaspoon ; drain and season the insides.

Chop the whites of the hard-boiled eggs and mix with the celery. Sieve the cheese and work half with the cream in a bowl. Combine celery mixture with this cheese and fill into the tomatoes ; replace the tops of the tomatoes 'on the slant'. Work the French dressing into the remaining cheese and add the chives.

Sieve the egg yolks on to a serving dish, set tomatoes on top and spoon over the dressing.

Stuffed tomatoes valaisannes

6 large tomatoes
$7\frac{1}{2}$ fl oz milk
cayenne pepper
nutmeg
1 oz butter
1 oz plain flour
3 egg yolks
$\frac{1}{2}$ oz Gruyère cheese (grated)
2 egg whites
salt and pepper
chopped chives
white wine

Method

Scald, skin and cut off the tops of the tomatoes, scoop out the seeds and drain tomatoes thoroughly. Heat the milk, seasoning it well with cayenne and nutmeg.

To make soufflé-type filling, prepare a very thick béchamel sauce with the butter and flour and the seasoned milk. Beat in the egg yolks one at a time, followed by the grated cheese. Allow it to cool.

Whip the egg whites until stiff and fold into the sauce.

Season the tomatoes and sprinkle over a little chopped chives. Set the tomatoes close together in a gratin dish and sprinkle them with white wine. Pipe the soufflé mixture into the tomatoes and bake in oven pre-set at 350°F or Mark 4, for about 20 minutes.

Tomatoes au gratin

1 lb ripe tomatoes
2-3 medium to large potatoes
3 large onions (preferably Spanish)
1-2 oz butter, or 1-2 tablespoons oil (for frying)
salt and pepper
1 rounded tablespoon chopped mixed herbs (tarragon, lemon thyme, marjoram)
1 rounded tablespoon chopped parsley
browned breadcrumbs

Method

Set the oven at 350°F or Mark 4. Skin the tomatoes and slice thickly. Boil the potatoes in their skins and then peel and cut into thin slices. Slice the onion and fry in butter (or oil) until nicely brown.

Take an ovenproof dish, put in a layer of tomatoes, then a layer of fried onion, then a layer of potato. Season this and scatter over half the herbs and parsley. Repeat these layers once again with the rest of the ingredients, pour over any fat left in the frying pan, then sprinkle with the crumbs. Put into the pre-set oven on the top shelf and bake for 25-30 minutes.

Tomato tart

For rich shortcrust pastry
8 oz plain flour
pinch of salt
4 oz butter
2 oz lard
1 egg yolk
2-3 tablespoons water

For filling
8 tomatoes
4½ oz browned breadcrumbs
6 oz grated cheese (Cheddar, or Gruyère)
¼ pint double cream
1 tablespoon chopped mixed herbs and parsley
1 dessertspoon anchovy essence
salt and pepper
grate of nutmeg (optional)

8-9 inch diameter flan ring

Method

Make up the pastry and chill well. Line it into the flan ring, making sure that there is a good edge standing up ¼ inch above the ring. Prick the bottom with a fork and set aside to chill. Set the oven at 400°F or Mark 6.

Meanwhile prepare the filling : scald and skin the tomatoes, cut them in half, remove the stalk and seeds. Sprinkle tomatoes well with salt and leave them to stand for about 30 minutes. Tip off any liquid and dry the halves well.

Scatter the browned crumbs into the bottom of the flan, arrange the tomatoes on top in a single layer, rounded sides uppermost, mix the cheese and cream together with the herbs and anchovy essence. Season well and add a little grating of nutmeg. Spoon this mixture over the tomatoes and bake tart in the pre-set oven for 30-40 minutes.

If the tart is browning too quickly after 25 minutes, lower the oven to 350°F or Mark 4 and continue to cook until the pastry shrinks slightly from the flan ring. Then remove the ring, and put the tart back into the oven for a few minutes. Serve hot or cold.

Turnips gratinés

1½ lb small turnips
2 oz butter
sprig of rosemary
1 lb potatoes (puréed) — see page 92
salt and pepper
½ onion (grated)

To serve
juice of ½ lemon
noisette butter

Method

Peel the turnips and boil until tender (10-15 minutes), then scoop out the centres, leaving the outer part as a 'cup'. Fry the bottoms of the 'cups' in 1 oz butter, adding the rosemary to the pan ; purée the scooped-out turnip, then add to the potato purée. Season well and fill mixture into turnip 'cups'. Arrange in a gratin dish, dot with rest of butter and sprinkle over the grated onion. Brown in the oven, pre-set at 400°F or Mark 6, for about 5-10 minutes. Pour over the lemon juice and noisette butter just before serving.

Turnips with onions

1½ lb small turnips
1 lb medium-size onions
2 oz butter
salt
pepper (ground from mill)

Small turnips, if dug up when no larger than a golf ball, can taste nutty and very sweet. Serve this recipe as an accompaniment to roasts.

Method

Peel the turnips and cut in ¼-inch slices ; cook until tender in boiling salted water, then drain. Slice the onions in thin rings and lightly brown them in the butter. Add onions to the turnips with seasoning and mix them together carefully. Serve hot.

Turnip salad

1 lb small turnips
1 large Spanish onion
salt and pepper
1 tablespoon soft brown sugar
2 tablespoons white wine vinegar
3 tablespoons olive oil
1 tablespoon grated horseradish
1 tablespoon double cream

This dish should be served as an accompaniment to cold roast beef.

Method

Peel and grate the turnips. Chop the onion very finely and then mix with turnip in a bowl. Mix seasoning, sugar and vinegar together, whisk in the oil and add the horseradish mixed with the cream. Pour this mixture over the vegetables, stir well, cover the bowl and chill salad for 24 hours before serving.

Ratatouille

½ lb courgettes
1-2 aubergines
½ lb, or 1 medium-size can, tomatoes
1 large green pepper
1 large red pepper
2 small onions (finely sliced into rings)
2 cloves of garlic (chopped) — optional
4 tablespoons olive oil
salt and pepper

Serve with steak or chops.

Method

Slice and salt the courgettes and aubergines and set aside. Scald, skin and remove seeds of fresh tomatoes and slice roughly, or drain canned ones. Halve the peppers, removing core and seeds, and cut into fine shreds.

Heat the oil in a stewpan, and fry the onion rings and garlic for 2-3 minutes. Wipe dry the courgettes and aubergines, add them to the pan and fry for 2-3 minutes on each side, adding extra oil as needed. Season the mixture, add shredded peppers and tomatoes, cover the pan and cook gently for a good hour or more on top of the stove, or in the oven, pre-set at 350°F or Mark 4. The ratatouille should cook down to a soft, rich mass.

Vegetables in béchamel sauce

For this excellent dish make a selection of three or four vegetables. Cook them as given below, arrange in a fireproof dish and cover with buttered paper or foil to keep hot, or when reheating.

Either of the béchamel sauces given in the appendix may be used. The long method is especially suitable for vegetables on their own since it is very delicate in flavour, although not as simple to make as the short method. Just before serving the dish, spoon over the sauce, which should be very creamy and thin enough in consistency for the shape and colour of the vegetables to show through.

Method

Cauliflower : break into sprigs and cook uncovered in boiling salted water for about 8-10 minutes, or until just tender. Drain, refresh and turn gently in a little melted butter.

Sprouts : cook until just tender in boiling, salted water for about 8 minutes, drain and toss in $\frac{1}{4}$ oz butter.

Carrots : keep whole, if young, otherwise quarter them lengthways. For about $1\frac{1}{2}$lb, just cover with cold water, add $\frac{1}{2}$ teaspoon salt, $\frac{1}{2}$ teaspoon caster sugar and $\frac{1}{2}$oz butter.

Cook carrots covered until tender, remove lid and boil until water has completely evaporated, leaving a sticky glaze. Sprinkle with a little finely chopped mint.

Button onions : for 8 oz, blanch, cook slowly in covered pan in $\frac{1}{2}$ oz butter, with 1 teaspoon caster sugar, until brown and sticky (8-10 minutes).

Mushrooms : keep whole, or quarter if large. Cook quickly in butter with a squeeze of lemon juice. Then drain on absorbent paper.

Whole, small tomatoes : skin and cook, covered, in a little butter until just tender.

Celery : cut stalks into 3-inch lengths, tie in bundles and cook until tender. Drain well and pour over a little melted butter.

Jardinière platter

$1\frac{1}{2}$ lb carrots
$1\frac{1}{2}$ lb small brussels sprouts (trimmed)
1 lb small pickling onions (skinned)
2 lb jerusalem artichokes (peeled), or 1 lb courgettes
$\frac{1}{2}$ lb button mushrooms
2 cauliflowers

For serving
3 teaspoons caster sugar (for carrots and onions)
1 teaspoon chopped mint (for carrots
$3\frac{3}{4}$ oz butter
juice of $\frac{1}{2}$ small lemon
salt and pepper
1 dessertspoon chopped parsley

The vegetables are all cooked separately and then arranged together on a large serving platter.

Method

Carrots : cook as opposite.

Brussels sprouts : cook as opposite.

Pickling onions : cover with cold water and bring to the boil — drain well. Return to the pan with 1 oz butter, 2 teaspoons caster sugar ; cover and cook slowly until they are brown and sticky. Shake the pan from time to time and turn the onions. They should be tender after 8-10 minutes' cooking, but this does depend on the speed of cooking.

Jerusalem artichokes : cut into even-size pieces after peeling and cook in boiling salted water with a slice of lemon to help keep their colour and to give flavour. When tender, drain artichokes well and add $\frac{1}{2}$ oz butter to the pan with pepper ground from the mill and a little extra salt to season.

Courgettes : thickly slice and blanch the courgettes in boiling water for 1 minute. Drain and return to the pan with $\frac{1}{2}$ oz butter, cover pan tightly and cook until tender for about 8-10 minutes.

Mushrooms : cook as opposite.

Cauliflower : cook as opposite.

To dish up, arrange the vegetables in rows in a large hot serving platter. Melt $1\frac{1}{2}$ oz butter in a small pan and cook slowly until a nut-brown, add the lemon juice, salt and pepper and the chopped parsley. Pour this butter, while it is still foaming, over the vegetables, particularly the artichokes (or courgettes) and the cauliflower.

Vegetable pie

- 6 oz quantity of shortcrust pastry
- 1 lb cooked vegetables (as good a variety as possible)
- 2 oz cooked haricot, or butter, beans
- 2 tomatoes (sliced)
- ½ pint brown sauce (made from vegetable liquor)
- little water

Pie dish (1½ pints capacity)

Method

Set the oven at 425°F or Mark 7. Cut up the vegetables and put them in pie dish with the beans. Place the sliced tomatoes on top and coat with the brown sauce. Cover the pie with the pastry and brush with water. Bake in the pre-set hot oven for 30 minutes or until brown.

Note : this pie can be covered with mashed potato instead of pastry. The same basic mixture can also be made up as a pudding to be covered with suet crust pastry and steamed for 2 hours.

Tarte primeurs

For rich shortcrust pastry
8 oz plain flour
$2\frac{1}{2}$ oz butter
$2\frac{1}{2}$ oz shortening
1 egg yolk
cold water (to mix)

selection of the following vegetables: French beans, carrots, onions, cucumber, tomatoes
$\frac{1}{2}$ oz butter
$\frac{3}{4}$ pint béchamel sauce (made with $1\frac{1}{4}$ oz butter, scant $1\frac{1}{4}$ oz flour and $\frac{3}{4}$ pint flavoured milk)
2-3 tablespoons cream

8-inch diameter flan ring

Method

Set oven at 375°F or Mark 5. Prepare the shortcrust pastry and line it into the flan case and bake blind.

Meanwhile prepare and cook the vegetables. Boil the beans ; cook the carrots and onions in $\frac{1}{2}$oz butter and very little water until tender. Dégorgé the cucumbers and sauté with the tomatoes.

Make the béchamel sauce, and, after simmering for 5-6 minutes, add the cream.

Pour a little of this sauce into the flan case, arrange vegetables on the top and coat with the remaining sauce.

Vegetarian chop suey

$\frac{1}{2}$ head of celery (diced)
$\frac{1}{2}$ small cabbage (diced)
2 large onions, or leeks (sliced)
2 large carrots (sliced)
3 tablespoons oil
1 cup vegetable stock
$\frac{1}{2}$ teaspoon yeast extract
$\frac{1}{2}$ teaspoon soy, or Worcestershire, sauce
$1\frac{1}{2}$-2 tablespoons cornflour
4 tablespoons water
salt
$\frac{1}{4}$ lb bean sprouts, or 1 small can (drained)

Method

Heat the oil in a large pan, add all the vegetables except the bean sprouts and sauté them for 3-5 minutes. Add the stock and bring to the boil. Simmer for 5 minutes, add the yeast extract and the soy (or Worcestershire) sauce. Mix the cornflour and water, add to the vegetables, season and cook for another 3-5 minutes. Add the bean sprouts and cook for a further 2 minutes. Serve with boiled rice.

Summer croustade

For croustade
about ½ loaf white bread (1-2 days old)
1-2 cloves of garlic (optional)
½ teaspoon salt
2 oz butter

For filling
mixed summer vegetables, ie. peas, broad beans, baby carrots, new potatoes, new beetroots
2-3 tablespoons French dressing (for marinating vegetables)
finely chopped mixed herbs
any good cream dressing (to be handed separately)

Method

Set the oven at 400°F or Mark 6. Chop the garlic (if using) and crush with the salt and then cream this into the butter. Cut the bread into thin slices, and then into 3-inch squares ; remove the crusts and discard. Spread with butter.

Butter a deep sandwich tin, or use a buttered ovenproof dish which can be taken directly to the table, and arrange bread squares, slightly overlapping, cornerwise around the edge so that one corner will project above the top of the tin. Cover the bottom of the tin with more squares, also overlapping, and then fit another smaller tin or dish inside the lined one to keep the bread in place. Bake in the pre-set moderately hot oven for 30-40 minutes or until golden-brown.

Take out the croustade (baked bread case), allow to cool and turn out of the tin very carefully (or leave in the oven-proof dish). Prepare and cook vegetables ; marinate each kind (while still hot) in French dressing for an hour or so. Lay the croustade on a flat dish (if turned out) and drain the vegetables of their marinade. Arrange them neatly in the croustade ; scatter over the finely chopped herbs. Serve cold with cream dressing handed separately.

Appendix

Notes and basic recipes

Almonds

Buy them with their skins on. This way they retain their oil better. Blanching to remove the skins gives extra juiciness.

To blanch : pour boiling water over the shelled nuts, cover the pan and leave until cool. Then the skins can be easily removed (test one with finger and thumb). Drain, rinse in cold water, press skins off with fingers. Rinse, dry thoroughly.

Anchovy butter

Soften 2 oz unsalted butter on a plate with a palette knife. Crush or pound 5-6 anchovy fillets (previously soaked in milk to remove excess salt), and add these to the butter with black pepper ground from the mill, together with 2 teaspoons anchovy essence to strengthen the flavour and give a delicate pink colour.

Boiled dressing

1 tablespoon caster sugar
1 dessertspoon plain flour
1 teaspoon salt
1 dessertspoon made mustard
1 tablespoon water
$\frac{1}{4}$ pint each vinegar and water (mixed)
1 egg
$\frac{1}{2}$ oz butter
cream, or creamy milk

Method

Mix dry ingredients together, add mustard and about 1 tablespoon of water. Add to vinegar and water and cook thoroughly for about 5 minutes.

Beat egg, add butter, pour on the hot vinegar mixture and beat thoroughly.

When cold dilute with cream or milk and mix well. This dressing keeps well, covered, in a refrigerator.

Breadcrumbs

Fresh white crumbs : take a large loaf (the best type to use is a sandwich loaf) at least two days old. Cut off the crust and keep to one side. Break up bread into crumbs either by rubbing through a wire sieve or a Mouli sieve, or by working in an electric blender.

Dried crumbs : make crumbs as above and spread on to a sheet of paper laid on a baking tin and cover with another sheet of paper to keep off any dust. Leave to dry in a warm temperature — the plate rack, or warming drawer, or the top of the oven, or even the airing cupboard, is ideal. The crumbs may take a day or two to dry thoroughly, and they must be crisp before storing. To make them uniformly fine, sift them through a wire bowl strainer.

Browned crumbs : bake crusts in a slow oven until golden-brown, then crush or grind them through a mincer. Sift crumbs through a wire bowl strainer to make them uniformly fine.

Store all crumbs in a dry, screw top jar.

Deep fat frying

Choose a deep, heavy gauge pan (fat bath or deep fryer) which covers source of heat, complete with a wire basket to fit. Or buy a separate folding wire basket for fitting into any saucepan (which must, however, be of reasonably heavy gauge because fat is heated to high temperatures in deep fat frying). This separate basket is useful when only occasionally deep fat frying because its flexibility means it can be used in a ordinary frying pan for cooking small foods such as croûtons.

When frying foods coated in soft batter mixture, you may find it easier to fry them in a fat bath without using a wire basket since batter tends to stick to the basket.

Suitable fats to use are : vegetable or nut oil ; lard, clarified dripping or commercially prepared fat, but it is better not to mix these. Olive oil and margarine are not suitable for deep frying. Never fill pan with more than one-third fat or oil.

Melt the fat, or put the oil, over moderate heat, then increase heat until right cooking temperature is reached. Oil must never be heated above 375°F, and for sunflower oil, and some commercially prepared fats (eg. Spry, Cookeen) 360°F is the highest recommended temperature. It is important to remember that oil does not 'haze' as solid fats do, until heated to a much higher temperature than is required — or is safe — for frying.

Apart from food cooked on a rising temperature, the fat or oil should never be below 340°F, as it is essential that the surface of the food is sealed immediately. This means it does not absorb fat, and is more digestible.

The best way of testing temperature is with a frying thermometer. Before using, it should be stood in a pan of hot water then carefully dried before putting into the fat bath. The hot water warms the glass so that it does not break when plunged into the hot fat.

If you have no thermometer, drop in a small piece of the food to be cooked (eg. a chip). If the fat or oil is at the right temperature, the food will rise immediately to the top and bubbles appear round it. Afternatively drop in a cube of day-old bread, which should turn golden-brown in 20 seconds at 375°F ; 60 seconds at 360°F.

French dressing

Mix 1 tablespoon wine, or tarragon, vinegar with ½ teaspoon each of salt and freshly ground black pepper. Add 3 tablespoons of salad oil.

When dressing thickens, taste for correct seasoning ; if it is sharp yet oily, add more salt. Quantities should be in the ratio of 1 part vinegar to 3 parts oil.

For **vinaigrette dressing** add freshly chopped herbs of choice.

Fritter batter

4 tablespoons plain flour
pinch of salt
2 egg yolks
1 tablespoon melted butter, or oil
¼ pint milk
1 egg white

Method

Sift flour with salt into a bowl, make a well in centre of flour, add egg yolks, melted butter, or oil, and mix with milk to a smooth batter ; beat thoroughly. Stand in a cool place for 30 minutes. Just before frying, whisk egg white stiffly and fold into batter. Fry in deep fat or up to ½-inch depth for shallow frying.

Gelatine

As gelatine setting strength varies according to brand, it is essentiel to follow instructions given on the pack. For instance Davis gelatine recommend 1 oz to set 2 pints of liquid.

Mayonnaise

2 egg yolks
salt and pepper
dry mustard
¾ cup of salad oil
2 tablespoons wine vinegar

This recipe will make ½ pint of mayonnaise.

Method
Work egg yolks and seasonings with a small whisk or wooden spoon in a bowl until thick ; then start adding the oil drop by drop. When 2 tablespoons of oil have been added this mixture will be very thick. Now carefully stir in 1 teaspoon of the vinegar.

The remaining oil can then be added a little more quickly, either 1 tablespoon at a time and beaten thoroughly between each addition until it is absorbed, or in a thin steady stream if you are using an electric beater.

When all the oil has been absorbed, add remaining vinegar to taste and extra salt and pepper as necessary.

To thin and lighten mayonnaise add a little hot water. For a coating consistency, thin with a little cream or milk.

Eggs should not come straight from the refrigerator. If oil is cloudy or chilled, it can be slightly warmed, which will lessen the chances of eggs curdling. Put oil bottle in a pan of hot water for a short time.

Watchpoint Great care must be taken to prevent mayonnaise curdling. Add oil drop by drop at first and then continue adding it very slowly.

Omelet

4 eggs
1½ tablespoons cold water
salt
black pepper (ground from mill)
1 oz butter

7-8 inch diameter omelet pan

Method
Break eggs into a basin and beat well with a fork. When well mixed, add water and seasoning (this should be done just before making it). Heat pan on medium heat. Put in butter in two pieces and, when frothing, pour in egg mixture at once. Leave 10-15 seconds before stirring round slowly with the flat of a fork. Do this once or twice round pan, stop and leave for another 5-6 seconds.

Lift up edge of omelet to let any remaining raw egg run on to hot pan. Now tilt pan away from you and fold over omelet to far side. Change your grip on pan so that the handle runs up the palm of your hand. Take the hot dish or plate, in your other hand, tilt it slightly and tip omelet on to it. Serve at once.

Pancake batter

4 oz plain flour
pinch of salt
1 egg
1 egg yolk
½ pint milk
1 tablespoon melted butter, or salad oil

Method
Sift the flour with the salt into a bowl, make a well in the centre, add the egg and yolk and begin to add the milk slowly, stirring all the time. When half the milk has been added, stir in the melted butter or oil and beat well until smooth.

Add the remaining milk and leave to stand for 30 minutes before using. The batter should have the consistency of thin cream — if too thick, add a little extra milk.

To cook the pancakes, wipe out the pan before setting over moderate heat. When thoroughly hot put in a few drops of oil. Take 1 tablespoon of the butter and tip this in the pan, rolling it round to coat the bottom evenly. Cook until underneath is a good brown than flip the pancake over with a palette knife and cook for about 10 seconds on the other side.

Pastry

Note : when terms such as 8 oz pastry or an 8 oz quantity of pastry are used, this means the amount obtained by using 8 oz of flour, not 8 oz of prepared dough.

Puff pastry

8 oz plain flour
pinch of salt
8 oz butter
1 teaspoon lemon juice
scant $\frac{1}{4}$ pint water (ice cold)

Method

Sift flour and salt into a bowl. Rub in a piece of butter the size of a walnut. Add lemon juice to water, make a well in centre of flour and pour in about two-thirds of the liquid. Mix with a palette, or round-bladed, knife. When the dough is beginning to form, add remaining water.

Turn out the dough on to a marble slab, a laminated-plastic work top, or a board, dusted with flour. Knead dough for 2-3 minutes, then roll out to a square about $\frac{1}{2}$-$\frac{3}{4}$ inch thick.

Beat butter, if necessary, to make it pliable and place in centre of dough. Fold this up over butter to enclose it completely (sides and ends over centre like a parcel). Wrap in a cloth or piece of greaseproof paper and put in the refrigerator for 10-15 minutes.

Flour slab or work top, put on dough, the join facing upwards, and bring rolling pin down on to dough 3-4 times to flatten it slightly.

Now roll out to a rectangle about $\frac{1}{2}$-$\frac{3}{4}$ inch thick. Fold into three, ends to middle, as accurately as possible, if necessary pulling the ends to keep them rectangular. Seal the edges with your hand or rolling pin and turn pastry half round to bring the edge towards you. Roll out again and fold in three (keep a note of the 'turns' given). Set pastry aside in refrigerator for 15 minutes.

Repeat this process, giving a total of 6 turns with a 15-minute rest after each two turns. Then leave in the refrigerator until wanted.

Rich shortcrust pastry

8 oz plain flour
pinch of salt
6 oz butter
1 rounded dessertspoon caster sugar (for sweet pastry)
1 egg yolk
2-3 tablespoons cold water

Method

Sift the flour with a pinch of salt into a mixing bowl. Drop in the butter and cut it into the flour until the small pieces are well coated. Then rub them in with the fingertips until the mixture looks like fine breadcrumbs. Stir in the sugar, mix egg yolk with water, tip into the fat and flour and mix quickly with a palette knife to a firm dough.

Turn on to a floured board and knead lightly till smooth. If possible, chill in refrigerator (wrapped in greaseproof paper, a polythene bag or foil) for 30 minutes before using.

Shortcrust pastry

8 oz plain flour
pinch of salt
4-6 oz butter, margarine, lard or shortening (one of the commercially prepared fats), or a mixture of any two
3-4 tablespoons cold water

Method

Sift the flour with a pinch of salt

into a mixing bowl. Cut the fat into the flour with a round-bladed knife and, as soon as the pieces are well coated with flour, rub in with the fingertips until the mixture looks like fine breadcrumbs.

Make a well in the centre, add the water (reserving about 1 tablespoon) and mix quickly with a knife. Press together with the fingers, adding the extra water, if necessary to give a firm dough.

Turn on to a floured board, knead pastry lightly until smooth. Chill in refrigerator (wrapped in greaseproof paper, a polythene bag, or foil) for 30 minutes before using.

Baking blind

A flan case should be pre-cooked before filling with soft foods. Once the flan ring is lined with pastry, chill for about 30 minutes to ensure the dough is well set.

Now line the pastry with crumpled greaseproof paper, pressing it well into the dough at the bottom edge and sides.

Three-parts fill the flan with uncooked rice or beans (to hold the shape) and put into the oven to bake. An 8-inch diameter flan ring holding a 6-8 oz quantity of pastry should cook for about 26 minutes in an oven at 400°F or Mark 6.

After about 20 minutes of the cooking time take flan out of the oven and carefully remove the paper and rice, or beans. (Rice, or beans, may be used many times over for baking blind.) Replace the flan in the oven to complete cooking. The ring itself can either be taken off with the paper and rice, or removed after cooking. Once cooked, slide the flan on to a wire rack and then leave to cool.

Rice (boiled)

There are almost as many ways of cooking rice as there are cooks, so if you have your own well-tried method stick to it, but if you have problems, the following method is foolproof.

Shower the rice into a large pan of boiling, salted water, at least 3 quarts for 8 oz, and add a slice of lemon for flavour. Stir with a fork to prevent sticking and boil steadily for about 12 minutes until tender. Rice very quickly overcooks so watch its cooking time carefully.

To stop rice cooking, tip it quickly into a colander and drain, or pour ½ cup of cold water into the pan and drain in a colander.

Then pour over a jug of hot water to wash away any remaining starch, making several holes through the rice (with the handle of a wooden spoon) to help it drain more quickly. Turn on to a large meat dish and leave in a warm place dry.

Turn rice from time to time with a fork.

For easy reheating, spoon rice into a well buttered, shallow fireproof dish which should be small enough for the rice to fill it amply. Place a sheet of well-buttered paper over the top. The rice can then be reheated and served in this dish. Allow 30 minutes in the oven at 350°F or Mark 4.

Sauces

Béchamel sauce

(Long method)

1 oz butter
2 tablespoons flour
1 pint milk
1 bouquet garni
salt and pepper
pinch of grated nutmeg
1 tablespoon cream (optional)

For mirepoix
1 small onion
1 small carrot
½ stick of celery
1 oz butter

Method
Dice the vegetables finely, and melt the butter in a large thick pan. Add this mirepoix of vegetables to the pan and press a piece of buttered paper down on top. Cover and cook gently for 8-10 minutes, do not allow to colour. Now turn the mirepoix on to a plate.

To make the roux : melt the butter, stir in flour off the heat, blend in one-third of the milk and set aside. Scald remaining milk (by bringing quickly to the boil and removing from heat immediately) and pour on to the roux, whisking well at the same time. Add bouquet garni, seasoning and a little nutmeg.

Stir sauce over heat until it boils, then add mirepoix. Simmer in half-covered pan on low heat for 40 minutes, stirring from time to time. Then run the resulting sauce through a conical strainer, pressing lightly to remove juice. Return to a clean pan for reheating. This sauce may be finished with 1 tablespoon of cream.

(Short method)

¾ pint milk
slice of onion
6 peppercorns
1 blade of mace
1 bayleaf
1 oz butter
2 tablespoons plain flour
salt and pepper
1 tablespoon cream (optional)

Method
Infuse milk with onion and spices in a covered pan over a low heat for 5-7 minutes, but do not boil. Pour the milk into a basin and wipe the pan out.

To make the roux : melt the butter slowly, remove pan from heat and stir in the flour. Pour on at least one-third of the milk through a strainer and blend together with a wooden spoon. Then add the rest of the milk, season lightly, return to heat and stir until boiling. Boil for not more than 2 minutes, then taste for seasoning. The sauce may be finished with 1 tablespoon of cream.

Demi-glace (basic brown) sauce

3 tablespoons salad oil
1 small onion (finely diced)
1 small carrot (finely diced)
½ stick of celery (finely diced)
1 rounded tablespoon plain flour
1 teaspoon tomato purée
1 tablespoon mushroom peelings (chopped), or 1 mushroom
1 pint well-flavoured brown stock
bouquet garni
salt and pepper

Method
Heat a saucepan, put in the oil and then add diced vegetables (of which there should be no more than 3 tablespoons in all). Lower heat and cook gently until vegetables are on point of changing colour ; an indication of this is when they shrink slightly.

Mix in the flour and brown it slowly, stirring occasionally with a metal spoon and scraping the flour well from the bottom of the pan. When it is a good colour draw pan aside, cool a little, add tomato purée and chopped peelings or mushroom ¾ pint of cold stock, bouquet garni and seasonings.

Bring to the boil, partially cover pan and cook gently for about 35-40 minutes. Skim off any scum which rises to the surface during this time. Add half the reserved stock, bring again to boil and skim. Simmer for 5 minutes. Add rest of stock, bring to boil and skim again. **Watchpoint** Addition of cold stock accelerates rising of scum and so helps to clear the sauce.

Cook for a further 5 minutes, then strain, pressing vegetables gently to extract the juice. Rinse out the pan and return sauce to it. Partially cover and continue to cook gently until syrupy in consistency.

Maltaise sauce

2 egg yolks
3-4 oz butter (unsalted)
grated rind of ½, and juice of 1, orange
salt and pepper
1 dessertspoon lemon juice
1 teaspoon tomato purée
3 tablespoons double cream (lightly whipped)

Method

Cream yolks in a bowl with nut of butter and grated orange rind ; season. Stand bowl in a bain-marie over heat ; add orange, lemon juice and tomato purée. Whisk until thick, adding rest of the butter (slightly softened) by degrees. Remove bowl from heat, continue to whisk for a minute, then fold in the cream.

Watchpoint In this sauce there is a fair proportion of liquid, so make sure this begins to thicken before adding too much of the butter. Quite a strong heat is necessary to start this off. Once the sauce does begin to thicken, it will happen quickly, so be ready to take the bowl from the heat. The butter can then be added fairly rapidly.

Mornay (cheese) sauce

1-1½ oz (2-3 rounded tablespoons) grated cheese
½ teaspoon made mustard (French, or English)
½ pint well-seasoned white, or béchamel, sauce

The cheese can be a mixture of Gruyère and Parmesan or a dry Cheddar. If using Gruyère, which thickens sauce, reduce basic roux to ½ oz each butter and flour (1 tablespoon). If too thick, add a little milk.

Method

Make white or béchamel sauce, remove from heat and gradually stir in grated cheese. When well mixed, add mustard. Reheat but do not boil.

Tomato sauce

1 oz butter
1 rounded dessertspoon plain flour
½ pint stock, or water
1 lb tomatoes, or 1 can (15 oz) tomatoes
bouquet garni
salt and pepper
pinch of granulated sugar (to season)
1 teaspoon tomato purée (optional)

Method

Melt the butter in a pan, stir in the flour. Draw pan off the heat, blend in the stock or water and stir until boiling.

Cut the tomatoes in half (after wiping them if fresh), and squeeze to remove seeds. Strain seeds to obtain juice only. Place tomatoes and juice into the sauce and add bouquet garni. Season and add tomato purée to strengthen flavour it necessary. Cover pan and cook gently for 25-35 minutes until tomatoes are pulpy. Remove bouquet garni and turn sauce into a strainer. Press it through, return to the rinsed-out pan, adjust seasoning and boil gently for about 5 minutes or until it is the right consistency.

Watchpoint A tomato sauce must have a flowing consistency as opposed to a coating one. The appearance is improved by stiring in ½ oz butter just before serving. This will give the sauce a good gloss.

White sauce

¾ oz butter
1 rounded tablespoon plain flour
½ pint milk
salt and pepper

A white sauce is quick and easy, made in exactly the same way and with same proportions as béchamel, but the milk is not flavoured. It can be used as the base for cheese, onion or other sauces with pronounced flavour.

Method
Melt the butter in a small pan, remove from heat and stir in the flour. Blend in half the milk, then stir in the rest. Stir this over moderate heat until boiling, then boil gently for 1-2 minutes. Season to taste.

Stock

Brown bone stock

3 lb beef bones (or mixed beef / veal)
2 onions (quartered)
2 carrots (quartered)
1 stick of celery (sliced)
large bouquet garni
6 peppercorns
3-4 quarts water
salt

6-quart capacity saucepan, or small fish kettle

Method
Wipe bones but do not wash unless unavoidable. Put into a very large pan. Set on gentle heat and leave bones to fry gently for 15-20 minutes. Enough fat will come out from the marrow so do not add any to pan unless bones are very dry. After 10 minutes add the vegetables.

When bones and vegetables are just coloured, add herbs, peppercorns and the water, which should come up two-thirds above level of ingredients. Bring slowly to the boil, skimming occasionally, then half cover pan and simmer 4-5 hours, or until stock tastes strong and good.

Strain off and use bones again for a second boiling. Although this second stock will not be so strong as the first, it is good for soups and gravies. Use the first stock for brown sauces, sautés, casseroles, or where a **jellied stock** is required. For a strong beef broth, add 1 lb shin of beef to the pot halfway through the cooking.

White bone stock

This stock forms a basis for cream sauces, white stews, etc. It is made in the same way as brown bone stock, except that bones and vegetables are not browned before the water is added, and veal bones are used. Do not add the vegetables until the bones have come to the boil and fat has been skimmed off.

Vegetable stock

1 lb carrots
1 lb onions
½ head of celery
½ oz butter
3-4 peppercorns
1 teaspoon tomato purée
2 quarts water
salt

Method
Quarter vegetables, brown lightly in the butter in a large pan. Add peppercorns, tomato purée, water and salt. Bring to boil, cover pan

and simmer 2 hours or until the stock has a good flavour.

Chicken stock

This should ideally be made from the giblets (neck, gizzard, heart and feet, if available), but never the liver which imparts a bitter flavour. This is better kept for making pâté, or sautéd and used as a savoury. Dry fry the giblets with an onion, washed but not peeled, and cut in half. To dry fry, use a thick pan with a lid, with barely enough fat to cover the bottom. Allow the pan to get very hot before putting in the giblets and onion, cook on full heat until lightly coloured. Remove pan from heat before covering with 2 pints of cold water. Add a large pinch of salt, a few peppercorns and a bouquet garni (bayleaf, thyme, parsley) and simmer gently for 1-2 hours. Alternatively, make the stock when you cook the chicken by putting the giblets in the roasting tin around the chicken with the onion and herbs, and use the measured quantity of water.

Tomato pulp

In season, use rather ripe tomatoes ; at other times of the year it is better to use canned Italian tomatoes. To make ½ pint of pulp, take ¾ lb ripe tomatoes (seeds removed) or a 14 oz can. Put into a pan with a clove of lightly bruised garlic, a bayleaf, salt, pepper ground from the mill and a slice of onion. Add a nut of butter, cover and cook slowly to a thick pulp, about 10-15 minutes. When really thick, pass pulp through a strainer. Adjust the seasoning, adding a little sugar if it is too sharp.

Tomatoes (skinning and seeding)

To scald and skin tomatoes place them in a bowl, pour boiling water over them and count 12 before pouring off the hot water and replacing it with cold. The skin then comes off easily. Cut a slice from the top (not stalk end) of each tomato, reserve slices ; hold tomato in hollow of your palm, flick out seeds with the handle of a teaspoon, using the bowl of the spoon to detach the core. So much the better if the spoon is worn and therefore slightly sharp.

Glossary

Bain-marie (au) To cook at temperature just below boiling point in a bain-marie (a saucepan standing in a larger pan of simmering water). Used in the preparation of sauces, creams and food liable to spoil if cooked over direct heat. May be carried out in oven or on top of stove.

Baste To spoon hot fat / liquid over food as it roasts.

Blanch To whiten meats and remove strong tastes from vegetables by bringing to the boil from cold water and draining before further cooking. Green vegetables should be put into boiling water and cooked for up to 1 minute.

Bouquet garni A bunch of herbs, traditionally made up of 2-3 parsley stalks, a pinch of thyme and a bayleaf, tied with string if used in liquids which are later strained. Otherwise herbs are tied in a piece of muslin for easy removal before serving the dish.

Butter, clarified Butter which is heated gently until foaming, skimmed well and the clear, yellow liquid strained off, leaving the sediment (milk solids) behind.

Butter, kneaded Liaison of twice as much butter as flour worked together as paste, added in small pieces to thicken liquid (usually at end of cooking process).

Butter, noisette Butter (preferably clarified) cooked to nut-brown colour.

Dégorger To remove impurities and strong flavours before cooking. This can be done by : **1** Soaking food, eg. uncooked ham, in cold water for specified length of time. **2** Sprinkling sliced vegetables, eg cucumber, with salt, covering with heavy plate, leaving up to 1 hour, and pressing out excess liquid with a weighted plate.

Flour, seasoned Plain flour, to which salt and pepper have been added.

Lardons Small $\frac{1}{4}$ inch thick strips of fat about $1\frac{1}{2}$ inches long, cut from piece of larding bacon which is solid fat. They are used to give extra fat to cuts of meat that have little or none of their own to protect them from drying out during cooking.

Liaison Mixture for thickening / binding sauce / gravy / soup, eg. roux, egg yolks and cream, kneaded butter.

Marinate To soak raw meat / game / fish in cooked or raw spiced liquid (marinade) of wine, oil, herbs and vegetables for hours / days before cooking. This softens, tenderises and flavours, and a marinade can be used for final sauce. Use glass / glazed / enamel / stainless steel vessel to withstand effects of acid.

Mirepoix Basic preparation for flavouring braises and sauces. Diced vegetables, sweated (cooked gently for a few minutes in butter), to draw out flavour. Diced ham or bacon and bayleaf sometimes included.

Refresh To pour cold water over previously blanched and drained food. This sets vegetable colours, cleans meat and offal.

Reduce To boil down sauce or any liquid to concentrate flavour and thicken the consistency.

Roux Fat and flour liaison (mixture),

used as the basis of all flour sauces. The weight of fat should be slightly more than that of flour.

Rust Underside of ham or bacon rasher, on the side opposite the rind. It is often tough and strong flavoured, so should be cut off.

Sauté To brown food in butter or oil and butter. Sometimes cooking is completed in a 'small sauce' ie. one made on the food in the sauté pan.

Scald 1 To plunge into boiling water for easy peeling. **2** To heat a liquid, eg. milk, to just under boiling point.

Sweat To draw out flavour by cooking diced or sliced vegetables gently in a little melted butter in covered pan until softened (5-10 minutes).

Index